Mometrix
TEST PREPARATION

DSST®

Life-Span Developmental Psychology
Exam Secrets Study Guide

DSST is a registered trademark of Prometric LLC, which is not affiliated with Mometrix Test Preparation and does not endorse this product.

Dear Future Exam Success Story

First of all, **THANK YOU** for purchasing Mometrix study materials!

Second, congratulations! You are one of the few determined test-takers who are committed to doing whatever it takes to excel on your exam. **You have come to the right place.** We developed these study materials with one goal in mind: to deliver you the information you need in a format that's concise and easy to use.

In addition to optimizing your guide for the content of the test, we've outlined our recommended steps for breaking down the preparation process into small, attainable goals so you can make sure you stay on track.

We've also analyzed the entire test-taking process, identifying the most common pitfalls and showing how you can overcome them and be ready for any curveball the test throws you.

Standardized testing is one of the biggest obstacles on your road to success, which only increases the importance of doing well in the high-pressure, high-stakes environment of test day. Your results on this test could have a significant impact on your future, and this guide provides the information and practical advice to help you achieve your full potential on test day.

Your success is our success

We would love to hear from you! If you would like to share the story of your exam success or if you have any questions or comments in regard to our products, please contact us at **800-673-8175** or **support@mometrix.com**.

Thanks again for your business and we wish you continued success!

Sincerely,
The Mometrix Test Preparation Team

Need more help? Check out our flashcards at: http://MometrixFlashcards.com/DSST

Copyright © 2026 by Mometrix Media LLC. All rights reserved.
Written and edited by the Mometrix Exam Secrets Test Prep Team
Printed in the United States of America

TABLE OF CONTENTS

INTRODUCTION	1
SECRET KEY #1 – PLAN BIG, STUDY SMALL	2
SECRET KEY #2 – MAKE YOUR STUDYING COUNT	3
SECRET KEY #3 – PRACTICE THE RIGHT WAY	4
SECRET KEY #4 – PACE YOURSELF	6
SECRET KEY #5 – HAVE A PLAN FOR GUESSING	7
TEST-TAKING STRATEGIES	10
THE STUDY OF LIFESPAN DEVELOPMENT	15
BIOLOGICAL DEVELOPMENT THROUGHOUT THE LIFE SPAN	22
PERCEPTION, LEARNING, AND MEMORY	36
COGNITION AND LANGUAGE	45
DSST PRACTICE TEST	66
ANSWER KEY AND EXPLANATIONS	73
HOW TO OVERCOME TEST ANXIETY	78
ONLINE RESOURCES	84

Introduction

Thank you for purchasing this resource! You have made the choice to prepare yourself for a test that could have a huge impact on your future, and this guide is designed to help you be fully ready for test day. Obviously, it's important to have a solid understanding of the test material, but you also need to be prepared for the unique environment and stressors of the test, so that you can perform to the best of your abilities.

For this purpose, the first section that appears in this guide is the **Secret Keys**. We've devoted countless hours to meticulously researching what works and what doesn't, and we've boiled down our findings to the five most impactful steps you can take to improve your performance on the test. We start at the beginning with study planning and move through the preparation process, all the way to the testing strategies that will help you get the most out of what you know when you're finally sitting in front of the test.

We recommend that you start preparing for your test as far in advance as possible. However, if you've bought this guide as a last-minute study resource and only have a few days before your test, we recommend that you skip over the first two Secret Keys since they address a long-term study plan.

If you struggle with **test anxiety**, we strongly encourage you to check out our recommendations for how you can overcome it. Test anxiety is a formidable foe, but it can be beaten, and we want to make sure you have the tools you need to defeat it.

Secret Key #1 – Plan Big, Study Small

There's a lot riding on your performance. If you want to ace this test, you're going to need to keep your skills sharp and the material fresh in your mind. You need a plan that lets you review everything you need to know while still fitting in your schedule. We'll break this strategy down into three categories.

Information Organization

Start with the information you already have: the official test outline. From this, you can make a complete list of all the concepts you need to cover before the test. Organize these concepts into groups that can be studied together, and create a list of any related vocabulary you need to learn so you can brush up on any difficult terms. You'll want to keep this vocabulary list handy once you actually start studying since you may need to add to it along the way.

Time Management

Once you have your set of study concepts, decide how to spread them out over the time you have left before the test. Break your study plan into small, clear goals so you have a manageable task for each day and know exactly what you're doing. Then just focus on one small step at a time. When you manage your time this way, you don't need to spend hours at a time studying. Studying a small block of content for a short period each day helps you retain information better and avoid stressing over how much you have left to do. You can relax knowing that you have a plan to cover everything in time. In order for this strategy to be effective though, you have to start studying early and stick to your schedule. Avoid the exhaustion and futility that comes from last-minute cramming!

Study Environment

The environment you study in has a big impact on your learning. Studying in a coffee shop, while probably more enjoyable, is not likely to be as fruitful as studying in a quiet room. It's important to keep distractions to a minimum. You're only planning to study for a short block of time, so make the most of it. Don't pause to check your phone or get up to find a snack. It's also important to **avoid multitasking**. Research has consistently shown that multitasking will make your studying dramatically less effective. Your study area should also be comfortable and well-lit so you don't have the distraction of straining your eyes or sitting on an uncomfortable chair.

The time of day you study is also important. You want to be rested and alert. Don't wait until just before bedtime. Study when you'll be most likely to comprehend and remember. Even better, if you know what time of day your test will be, set that time aside for study. That way your brain will be used to working on that subject at that specific time and you'll have a better chance of recalling information.

Finally, it can be helpful to team up with others who are studying for the same test. Your actual studying should be done in as isolated an environment as possible, but the work of organizing the information and setting up the study plan can be divided up. In between study sessions, you can discuss with your teammates the concepts that you're all studying and quiz each other on the details. Just be sure that your teammates are as serious about the test as you are. If you find that your study time is being replaced with social time, you might need to find a new team.

Secret Key #2 – Make Your Studying Count

You're devoting a lot of time and effort to preparing for this test, so you want to be absolutely certain it will pay off. This means doing more than just reading the content and hoping you can remember it on test day. It's important to make every minute of study count. There are two main areas you can focus on to make your studying count.

Retention

It doesn't matter how much time you study if you can't remember the material. You need to make sure you are retaining the concepts. To check your retention of the information you're learning, try recalling it at later times with minimal prompting. Try carrying around flashcards and glance at one or two from time to time or ask a friend who's also studying for the test to quiz you.

To enhance your retention, look for ways to put the information into practice so that you can apply it rather than simply recalling it. If you're using the information in practical ways, it will be much easier to remember. Similarly, it helps to solidify a concept in your mind if you're not only reading it to yourself but also explaining it to someone else. Ask a friend to let you teach them about a concept you're a little shaky on (or speak aloud to an imaginary audience if necessary). As you try to summarize, define, give examples, and answer your friend's questions, you'll understand the concepts better and they will stay with you longer. Finally, step back for a big picture view and ask yourself how each piece of information fits with the whole subject. When you link the different concepts together and see them working together as a whole, it's easier to remember the individual components.

Finally, practice showing your work on any multi-step problems, even if you're just studying. Writing out each step you take to solve a problem will help solidify the process in your mind, and you'll be more likely to remember it during the test.

Modality

Modality simply refers to the means or method by which you study. Choosing a study modality that fits your own individual learning style is crucial. No two people learn best in exactly the same way, so it's important to know your strengths and use them to your advantage.

For example, if you learn best by visualization, focus on visualizing a concept in your mind and draw an image or a diagram. Try color-coding your notes, illustrating them, or creating symbols that will trigger your mind to recall a learned concept. If you learn best by hearing or discussing information, find a study partner who learns the same way or read aloud to yourself. Think about how to put the information in your own words. Imagine that you are giving a lecture on the topic and record yourself so you can listen to it later.

For any learning style, flashcards can be helpful. Organize the information so you can take advantage of spare moments to review. Underline key words or phrases. Use different colors for different categories. Mnemonic devices (such as creating a short list in which every item starts with the same letter) can also help with retention. Find what works best for you and use it to store the information in your mind most effectively and easily.

Secret Key #3 – Practice the Right Way

Your success on test day depends not only on how many hours you put into preparing, but also on whether you prepared the right way. It's good to check along the way to see if your studying is paying off. One of the most effective ways to do this is by taking practice tests to evaluate your progress. Practice tests are useful because they show exactly where you need to improve. Every time you take a practice test, pay special attention to these three groups of questions:

- The questions you got wrong
- The questions you had to guess on, even if you guessed right
- The questions you found difficult or slow to work through

This will show you exactly what your weak areas are, and where you need to devote more study time. Ask yourself why each of these questions gave you trouble. Was it because you didn't understand the material? Was it because you didn't remember the vocabulary? Do you need more repetitions on this type of question to build speed and confidence? Dig into those questions and figure out how you can strengthen your weak areas as you go back to review the material.

Additionally, many practice tests have a section explaining the answer choices. It can be tempting to read the explanation and think that you now have a good understanding of the concept. However, an explanation likely only covers part of the question's broader context. Even if the explanation makes perfect sense, **go back and investigate** every concept related to the question until you're positive you have a thorough understanding.

As you go along, keep in mind that the practice test is just that: practice. Memorizing these questions and answers will not be very helpful on the actual test because it is unlikely to have any of the same exact questions. If you only know the right answers to the sample questions, you won't be prepared for the real thing. **Study the concepts** until you understand them fully, and then you'll be able to answer any question that shows up on the test.

It's important to wait on the practice tests until you're ready. If you take a test on your first day of study, you may be overwhelmed by the amount of material covered and how much you need to learn. Work up to it gradually.

On test day, you'll need to be prepared for answering questions, managing your time, and using the test-taking strategies you've learned. It's a lot to balance, like a mental marathon that will have a big impact on your future. Like training for a marathon, you'll need to start slowly and work your way up. When test day arrives, you'll be ready.

Start with the strategies you've read in the first two Secret Keys—plan your course and study in the way that works best for you. If you have time, consider using multiple study resources to get different approaches to the same concepts. It can be helpful to see difficult concepts from more than one angle. Then find a good source for practice tests. Many times, the test website will suggest potential study resources or provide sample tests.

Practice Test Strategy

If you're able to find at least three practice tests, we recommend this strategy:

UNTIMED AND OPEN-BOOK PRACTICE

Take the first test with no time constraints and with your notes and study guide handy. Take your time and focus on applying the strategies you've learned.

TIMED AND OPEN-BOOK PRACTICE

Take the second practice test open-book as well, but set a timer and practice pacing yourself to finish in time.

TIMED AND CLOSED-BOOK PRACTICE

Take any other practice tests as if it were test day. Set a timer and put away your study materials. Sit at a table or desk in a quiet room, imagine yourself at the testing center, and answer questions as quickly and accurately as possible.

Keep repeating timed and closed-book tests on a regular basis until you run out of practice tests or it's time for the actual test. Your mind will be ready for the schedule and stress of test day, and you'll be able to focus on recalling the material you've learned.

Secret Key #4 – Pace Yourself

Once you're fully prepared for the material on the test, your biggest challenge on test day will be managing your time. Just knowing that the clock is ticking can make you panic even if you have plenty of time left. Work on pacing yourself so you can build confidence against the time constraints of the exam. Pacing is a difficult skill to master, especially in a high-pressure environment, so **practice is vital**.

Set time expectations for your pace based on how much time is available. For example, if a section has 60 questions and the time limit is 30 minutes, you know you have to average 30 seconds or less per question in order to answer them all. Although 30 seconds is the hard limit, set 25 seconds per question as your goal, so you reserve extra time to spend on harder questions. When you budget extra time for the harder questions, you no longer have any reason to stress when those questions take longer to answer.

Don't let this time expectation distract you from working through the test at a calm, steady pace, but keep it in mind so you don't spend too much time on any one question. Recognize that taking extra time on one question you don't understand may keep you from answering two that you do understand later in the test. If your time limit for a question is up and you're still not sure of the answer, mark it and move on, and come back to it later if the time and the test format allow. If the testing format doesn't allow you to return to earlier questions, just make an educated guess; then put it out of your mind and move on.

On the easier questions, be careful not to rush. It may seem wise to hurry through them so you have more time for the challenging ones, but it's not worth missing one if you know the concept and just didn't take the time to read the question fully. Work efficiently but make sure you understand the question and have looked at all of the answer choices, since more than one may seem right at first.

Even if you're paying attention to the time, you may find yourself a little behind at some point. You should speed up to get back on track, but do so wisely. Don't panic; just take a few seconds less on each question until you're caught up. Don't guess without thinking, but do look through the answer choices and eliminate any you know are wrong. If you can get down to two choices, it is often worthwhile to guess from those. Once you've chosen an answer, move on and don't dwell on any that you skipped or had to hurry through. If a question was taking too long, chances are it was one of the harder ones, so you weren't as likely to get it right anyway.

On the other hand, if you find yourself getting ahead of schedule, it may be beneficial to slow down a little. The more quickly you work, the more likely you are to make a careless mistake that will affect your score. You've budgeted time for each question, so don't be afraid to spend that time. Practice an efficient but careful pace to get the most out of the time you have.

Secret Key #5 – Have a Plan for Guessing

When you're taking the test, you may find yourself stuck on a question. Some of the answer choices seem better than others, but you don't see the one answer choice that is obviously correct. What do you do?

The scenario described above is very common, yet most test takers have not effectively prepared for it. Developing and practicing a plan for guessing may be one of the single most effective uses of your time as you get ready for the exam.

In developing your plan for guessing, there are three questions to address:

- When should you start the guessing process?
- How should you narrow down the choices?
- Which answer should you choose?

When to Start the Guessing Process

Unless your plan for guessing is to select C every time (which, despite its merits, is not what we recommend), you need to leave yourself enough time to apply your answer elimination strategies. Since you have a limited amount of time for each question, that means that if you're going to give yourself the best shot at guessing correctly, you have to decide quickly whether or not you will guess.

Of course, the best-case scenario is that you don't have to guess at all, so first, see if you can answer the question based on your knowledge of the subject and basic reasoning skills. Focus on the key words in the question and try to jog your memory of related topics. Give yourself a chance to bring the knowledge to mind, but once you realize that you don't have (or you can't access) the knowledge you need to answer the question, it's time to start the guessing process.

It's almost always better to start the guessing process too early than too late. It only takes a few seconds to remember something and answer the question from knowledge. Carefully eliminating wrong answer choices takes longer. Plus, going through the process of eliminating answer choices can actually help jog your memory.

Summary: Start the guessing process as soon as you decide that you can't answer the question based on your knowledge.

How to Narrow Down the Choices

The next chapter in this book (**Test-Taking Strategies**) includes a wide range of strategies for how to approach questions and how to look for answer choices to eliminate. You will definitely want to read those carefully, practice them, and figure out which ones work best for you. Here though, we're going to address a mindset rather than a particular strategy.

Your odds of guessing an answer correctly depend on how many options you are choosing from.

Number of options left	5	4	3	2	1
Odds of guessing correctly	20%	25%	33%	50%	100%

You can see from this chart just how valuable it is to be able to eliminate incorrect answers and make an educated guess, but there are two things that many test takers do that cause them to miss out on the benefits of guessing:

- Accidentally eliminating the correct answer
- Selecting an answer based on an impression

We'll look at the first one here, and the second one in the next section.

To avoid accidentally eliminating the correct answer, we recommend a thought exercise called **the $5 challenge**. In this challenge, you only eliminate an answer choice from contention if you are willing to bet $5 on it being wrong. Why $5? Five dollars is a small but not insignificant amount of money. It's an amount you could afford to lose but wouldn't want to throw away. And while losing $5 once might not hurt too much, doing it twenty times will set you back $100. In the same way, each small decision you make—eliminating a choice here, guessing on a question there—won't by itself impact your score very much, but when you put them all together, they can make a big difference. By holding each answer choice elimination decision to a higher standard, you can reduce the risk of accidentally eliminating the correct answer.

The $5 challenge can also be applied in a positive sense: If you are willing to bet $5 that an answer choice *is* correct, go ahead and mark it as correct.

Summary: Only eliminate an answer choice if you are willing to bet $5 that it is wrong.

Which Answer to Choose

You're taking the test. You've run into a hard question and decided you'll have to guess. You've eliminated all the answer choices you're willing to bet $5 on. Now you have to pick an answer. Why do we even need to talk about this? Why can't you just pick whichever one you feel like when the time comes?

The answer to these questions is that if you don't come into the test with a plan, you'll rely on your impression to select an answer choice, and if you do that, you risk falling into a trap. The test writers know that everyone who takes their test will be guessing on some of the questions, so they intentionally write wrong answer choices to seem plausible. You still have to pick an answer though, and if the wrong answer choices are designed to look right, how can you ever be sure that you're not falling for their trap? The best solution we've found to this dilemma is to take the decision out of your hands entirely. Here is the process we recommend:

Once you've eliminated any choices that you are confident (willing to bet $5) are wrong, select the first remaining choice as your answer.

Whether you choose to select the first remaining choice, the second, or the last, the important thing is that you use some preselected standard. Using this approach guarantees that you will not be enticed into selecting an answer choice that looks right, because you are not basing your decision on how the answer choices look.

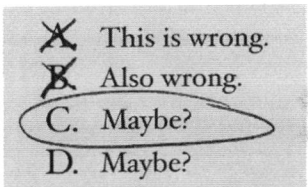

This is not meant to make you question your knowledge. Instead, it is to help you recognize the difference between your knowledge and your impressions. There's a huge difference between thinking an answer is right because of what you know, and thinking an answer is right because it looks or sounds like it should be right.

Summary: To ensure that your selection is appropriately random, make a predetermined selection from among all answer choices you have not eliminated.

Test-Taking Strategies

This section contains a list of test-taking strategies that you may find helpful as you work through the test. By taking what you know and applying logical thought, you can maximize your chances of answering any question correctly!

It is very important to realize that every question is different and every person is different: no single strategy will work on every question, and no single strategy will work for every person. That's why we've included all of them here, so you can try them out and determine which ones work best for different types of questions and which ones work best for you.

Question Strategies

⊘ READ CAREFULLY

Read the question and the answer choices carefully. Don't miss the question because you misread the terms. You have plenty of time to read each question thoroughly and make sure you understand what is being asked. Yet a happy medium must be attained, so don't waste too much time. You must read carefully and efficiently.

⊘ CONTEXTUAL CLUES

Look for contextual clues. If the question includes a word you are not familiar with, look at the immediate context for some indication of what the word might mean. Contextual clues can often give you all the information you need to decipher the meaning of an unfamiliar word. Even if you can't determine the meaning, you may be able to narrow down the possibilities enough to make a solid guess at the answer to the question.

⊘ PREFIXES

If you're having trouble with a word in the question or answer choices, try dissecting it. Take advantage of every clue that the word might include. Prefixes can be a huge help. Usually, they allow you to determine a basic meaning. *Pre-* means before, *post-* means after, *pro-* is positive, *de-* is negative. From prefixes, you can get an idea of the general meaning of the word and try to put it into context.

⊘ HEDGE WORDS

Watch out for critical hedge words, such as *likely, may, can, often, almost, mostly, usually, generally, rarely,* and *sometimes*. Question writers insert these hedge phrases to cover every possibility. Often an answer choice will be wrong simply because it leaves no room for exception. Be on guard for answer choices that have definitive words such as *exactly* and *always*.

⊘ SWITCHBACK WORDS

Stay alert for *switchbacks*. These are the words and phrases frequently used to alert you to shifts in thought. The most common switchback words are *but, although,* and *however*. Others include *nevertheless, on the other hand, even though, while, in spite of, despite,* and *regardless of*. Switchback words are important to catch because they can change the direction of the question or an answer choice.

ⓘ FACE VALUE

When in doubt, use common sense. Accept the situation in the problem at face value. Don't read too much into it. These problems will not require you to make wild assumptions. If you have to go beyond creativity and warp time or space in order to have an answer choice fit the question, then you should move on and consider the other answer choices. These are normal problems rooted in reality. The applicable relationship or explanation may not be readily apparent, but it is there for you to figure out. Use your common sense to interpret anything that isn't clear.

Answer Choice Strategies

ⓘ ANSWER SELECTION

The most thorough way to pick an answer choice is to identify and eliminate wrong answers until only one is left, then confirm it is the correct answer. Sometimes an answer choice may immediately seem right, but be careful. The test writers will usually put more than one reasonable answer choice on each question, so take a second to read all of them and make sure that the other choices are not equally obvious. As long as you have time left, it is better to read every answer choice than to pick the first one that looks right without checking the others.

ⓘ ANSWER CHOICE FAMILIES

An answer choice family consists of two (in rare cases, three) answer choices that are very similar in construction and cannot all be true at the same time. If you see two answer choices that are direct opposites or parallels, one of them is usually the correct answer. For instance, if one answer choice says that quantity *x* increases and another either says that quantity *x* decreases (opposite) or says that quantity *y* increases (parallel), then those answer choices would fall into the same family. An answer choice that doesn't match the construction of the answer choice family is more likely to be incorrect. Most questions will not have answer choice families, but when they do appear, you should be prepared to recognize them.

ⓘ ELIMINATE ANSWERS

Eliminate answer choices as soon as you realize they are wrong, but make sure you consider all possibilities. If you are eliminating answer choices and realize that the last one you are left with is also wrong, don't panic. Start over and consider each choice again. There may be something you missed the first time that you will realize on the second pass.

ⓘ AVOID FACT TRAPS

Don't be distracted by an answer choice that is factually true but doesn't answer the question. You are looking for the choice that answers the question. Stay focused on what the question is asking for so you don't accidentally pick an answer that is true but incorrect. Always go back to the question and make sure the answer choice you've selected actually answers the question and is not merely a true statement.

ⓘ EXTREME STATEMENTS

In general, you should avoid answers that put forth extreme actions as standard practice or proclaim controversial ideas as established fact. An answer choice that states the "process should be used in certain situations, if…" is much more likely to be correct than one that states the "process should be discontinued completely." The first is a calm rational statement and doesn't even make a definitive, uncompromising stance, using a hedge word *if* to provide wiggle room, whereas the second choice is far more extreme.

✓ BENCHMARK

As you read through the answer choices and you come across one that seems to answer the question well, mentally select that answer choice. This is not your final answer, but it's the one that will help you evaluate the other answer choices. The one that you selected is your benchmark or standard for judging each of the other answer choices. Every other answer choice must be compared to your benchmark. That choice is correct until proven otherwise by another answer choice beating it. If you find a better answer, then that one becomes your new benchmark. Once you've decided that no other choice answers the question as well as your benchmark, you have your final answer.

✓ PREDICT THE ANSWER

Before you even start looking at the answer choices, it is often best to try to predict the answer. When you come up with the answer on your own, it is easier to avoid distractions and traps because you will know exactly what to look for. The right answer choice is unlikely to be word-for-word what you came up with, but it should be a close match. Even if you are confident that you have the right answer, you should still take the time to read each option before moving on.

General Strategies

✓ TOUGH QUESTIONS

If you are stumped on a problem or it appears too hard or too difficult, don't waste time. Move on! Remember though, if you can quickly check for obviously incorrect answer choices, your chances of guessing correctly are greatly improved. Before you completely give up, at least try to knock out a couple of possible answers. Eliminate what you can and then guess at the remaining answer choices before moving on.

✓ CHECK YOUR WORK

Since you will probably not know every term listed and the answer to every question, it is important that you get credit for the ones that you do know. Don't miss any questions through careless mistakes. If at all possible, try to take a second to look back over your answer selection and make sure you've selected the correct answer choice and haven't made a costly careless mistake (such as marking an answer choice that you didn't mean to mark). This quick double check should more than pay for itself in caught mistakes for the time it costs.

✓ PACE YOURSELF

It's easy to be overwhelmed when you're looking at a page full of questions; your mind is confused and full of random thoughts, and the clock is ticking down faster than you would like. Calm down and maintain the pace that you have set for yourself. Especially as you get down to the last few minutes of the test, don't let the small numbers on the clock make you panic. As long as you are on track by monitoring your pace, you are guaranteed to have time for each question.

✓ DON'T RUSH

It is very easy to make errors when you are in a hurry. Maintaining a fast pace in answering questions is pointless if it makes you miss questions that you would have gotten right otherwise. Test writers like to include distracting information and wrong answers that seem right. Taking a little extra time to avoid careless mistakes can make all the difference in your test score. Find a pace that allows you to be confident in the answers that you select.

⊘ Keep Moving

Panicking will not help you pass the test, so do your best to stay calm and keep moving. Taking deep breaths and going through the answer elimination steps you practiced can help to break through a stress barrier and keep your pace.

Final Notes

The combination of a solid foundation of content knowledge and the confidence that comes from practicing your plan for applying that knowledge is the key to maximizing your performance on test day. As your foundation of content knowledge is built up and strengthened, you'll find that the strategies included in this chapter become more and more effective in helping you quickly sift through the distractions and traps of the test to isolate the correct answer.

Now that you're preparing to move forward into the test content chapters of this book, be sure to keep your goal in mind. As you read, think about how you will be able to apply this information on the test. If you've already seen sample questions for the test and you have an idea of the question format and style, try to come up with questions of your own that you can answer based on what you're reading. This will give you valuable practice applying your knowledge in the same ways you can expect to on test day.

Good luck and good studying!

The Study of Lifespan Development

LIFESPAN PERSPECTIVE
Unlike other approaches to developmental psychology, which often indicate that development ends during adulthood, the lifespan perspective emphasizes continuous progress until death. This perspective also suggests that development occurs in several dimensions: biology, intellect, attention, abstract thinking, and social skill. Development is multi-directional, according to this perspective. In other words, age and experience cause changes in all sorts of fields. The degree to which a person can change is called his plasticity of development. The lifespan perspective emphasizes that development occurs within the context of a person's family, community, religion, peer group, and society.

BASIC IDEAS OF FREUD AND ERIKSON
According to Freud, the first experiences in a person's life have a formative effect on his personality as an adult. In particular, the adult personality is formed by the resolution of the conflict between the desire for pleasure and the reality of insufficiency. For Freud, the sexual instinct is the primary motivator. Erikson, on the other hand, revised Freud's theory by expanding the sexual instinct into a more general desire for social interaction. Also contra Freud, Erikson suggested that personality development continues throughout life, rather than being restricted to the first five years.

FREUDIAN STAGES OF DEVELOPMENT
Sigmund Freud outlined five stages of psychosexual development: oral, anal, phallic, latency, and genital. During the oral stage, which lasts from birth to about 1.5 years of age, the child's primary focus of pleasure is his mouth. The anal stage lasts until the child is three years old, and is the stage in which the anus is the focus of pleasure. In the phallic stage, which runs from about the third to the sixth year, the child is preoccupied with his genitals. In the latency stage, which span from age six to puberty, sexual interest is put aside as the child's focus is on intellectual and social development. In puberty, however, which Freud called the genital stage, sexual interest reemerges and becomes focused on other people.

ERIKSON'S STAGES OF DEVELOPMENT
Erikson's stages of development are as follows:

- Year one: trust versus mistrust - During this stage, the child determines whether his environment is a positive or negative place.
- Years one to three: autonomy versus shame - A child begins to act independently, but may become doubtful if he is punished too much.
- Years four and five: initiative versus guilt - The child begins to seek out information and become responsible for his behavior.
- Year six to puberty: industry versus inferiority - The child begins to develop cognitive sophistication, though he may become discouraged.
- Adolescence: identity versus identity confusion - The child seeks to define his own identity.
- Early adulthood: intimacy versus isolation - The person begins to establish close relationships.
- Middle adulthood: generativity versus stagnation - The person either continues to move forward and become more socially integrated or is inert.
- Late adulthood: integrity versus despair - A person either solidifies a more complex personality or becomes overwhelmed by existential angst.

Maslow's Hierarchy of Needs

Psychologist Abraham Maslow listed human needs in terms of their relative importance. He depicted needs on a pyramid. The most important needs, at the base of the pyramid, must be satisfied before higher needs can be addressed. The needs at the bottom of the pyramid are things like shelter, food, water, and the desire for reproduction. After these needs are satisfied, a person can begin to address the needs for friendship, accomplishment, self-esteem, and community. At the very top of the pyramid is the need for self-actualization, which is the need to fully achieve personal potential.

Domains of Development

Developmental psychologists outline three fundamental domain of development: cognitive, physical, and emotional-social. Cognitive developments are changes in thinking and reasoning, including the development of abstract thought, linguistic ability, and memory. Physical development is the set of changes in the human body, including both maturation and degeneration. The brain's development as an organ is included in physical development. Emotional-social development, finally, is the set of personality changes that affect a person's emotional development and social skills.

Main Determinants of Development

Personal development occurs through biological, cognitive, and socio-emotional processes. Biological processes are most apparent to the eye. These include changes in appearance, as well as changes in the physical structure of the brain and internal organs. Cognitive processes, on the other hand, have to do with the growth and decline of the reasoning faculty, as well as the use of language and numbers. Finally, socioemotional processes relate to interpersonal communication and the regulation of the emotions. These processes have to do with changes in the way a person relates to others and the way in which a person can govern his own feelings.

Nature vs. Nurture

One of the fundamental debates in psychology is the extent to which human development is affected by heredity or environment. In the shorthand of psychology, this is known as the debate between nature and nurture. Advocates of the nature side believes that human development is regular and consistent, and motivated primarily by forces of biological change inside the human body. Those who take the nurture side, on the other hand, assert that the social and physical environments are the most important determinants of development. These professionals tend to focus on the influence of family, health, and community.

Mechanistic and Organismic Models of Development

Psychologists tend to either use the mechanistic or organismic model when discussing human development. According to the mechanistic model, human beings are merely physical objects in a well-ordered, logical universe. The mechanistic model of human development suggests that people change in gradual but continuous ways, in large part because of external influences. The organismic model, on the other hand, assigns much more agency to humans; it suggests that individuals are largely responsible for the changes in their own lives. The organismic model of human development declares that personal change occurs in discrete steps, and is not entirely motivated by external forces.

Continuity and Discontinuity Models of Development

According to the continuity model of human development, human beings change in steady, ongoing ways. Psychologists who subscribe to the continuity model of development believe that learning is a major determinant of behavior, and that learning occurs slowly over time. The discontinuity model, on the other hand, describes personality development as a series of defined stages, in which the ego and personae undergo measurable change. Famous versions of the discontinuity model include the developmental theories advanced by Piaget, Freud, and Erikson.

VYGOTSKY'S SOCIOCULTURAL COGNITIVE THEORY

The Russian developmental psychologist Lev Vygotsky asserted that social and cultural forces are the predominant influence on human development. Vygotsky is famous for the so-called socio-cultural cognitive theory, which identifies language as the fundamental driver of reason and memory. Moreover, adherents to this theory believe that an individual's social milieu exerts major influence on his thought processes. The society in which one develops suggests the form and content of both intellectual development and expression. For this reason, Vygotsky asserted that learning should be focused on the acquisition of cultural artifacts, like language, mnemonics, and mathematics.

CASE STUDY

In the case study method of data gathering, research focuses on a single person rather than on a collection of people. This is a form of longitudinal design, in which one subject is isolated, and often one special aspect of that person's life is studied in close detail. Of course, the results of a case study do not provide comparisons with other people. It is common for case studies to be tainted by the prejudices of the researcher, so results should be carefully studied before being accepted as valid.

LIMITATIONS

The most obvious problem with the case study approach to data gathering is that it isolates one person, and therefore cannot make descriptions about a population at large. Another potential problem is that over the course of the study the subject and the researcher will become so familiar that their relationship will taint the results of the study. For instance, the researcher may develop a positive or negative opinion about the subject, which may prejudice his research. It is very useful for case studies to involve a strict protocol and multiple researchers to guard against creeping bias by a particular individual.

CORRELATIONAL RESEARCH

Like descriptive research, correlational research is distinct from experimental research. Whereas descriptive research is mainly restricted to observation and record-keeping, correlational research aims at diagnosing the causal relationships between environment and behavior. For instance, a correlational research study might examine a link between caffeine consumption and aggressive behavior. As with descriptive research, correlational research issues intervention in the lives of the subject. However, the results of correlational research cannot be said to firmly establish causal relationships, as a broad array of factors can contribute to a specific behavior.

CORRELATIONAL ANALYSIS

Correlational analysis is used to draw links between the variables observed during a research study. It should be noted, however, that correlational analysis does not establish causal relationships between variables. In correlational analysis, numerical data is placed on a graph. The degree to which the variables correlate is known as the correlation coefficient. A correlational coefficient can range from -1.00, a perfect negative correlation, to +1.00, a perfect positive correlation. A perfect negative correlation means that when one variable occurs, the other variable never occurs. A perfect positive correlation means that when one variable occurs, the other variable always occurs as well.

CROSS-SECTIONAL DESIGN

Cross-sectional design is a form of research study in which the members of several different age groups are examined simultaneously. Usually, this type of study is performed to identify differences between people of various ages. For instance, an experiment might be aimed at identifying differences in memory between twenty-year-olds and fifty-year-olds. A cross-sectional design study can yield some of the same benefits as a longitudinal design study because it includes subjects of all different ages. In addition, it only requires one sampling session, and is therefore much easier to perform. Of course, this study does not allow researchers to use the same individuals over a long interval.

DISADVANTAGES

The main disadvantage of cross-sectional research is that it is extremely hard to find subject groups appropriate for comparison. Even a slight age difference can have a significant effect on the results, as the economic, social, and political trends in the country can exercise vastly different influences on the members of the population who are of a different age. The reactions to given external forces may be completely different for individuals of different generations. These differences related to age and background can sometimes make it difficult to isolate trends in cross-sectional design data. Indeed, this phenomenon of confusion is so common it has been given a name: confounding.

SEQUENTIAL DESIGN

Sequential design research is a sort of combination of the longitudinal and cross-sectional designs. In this design study, multiple age groups are evaluated over an interval. Sometimes, this interval is very long, like five or ten years. A sequential design study, then, both examines the same individuals over time and simultaneously compares individuals of different ages. These studies are not vulnerable to the singular events, as for instance major wars, that can affect longitudinal studies. Usually, a sequential design study can be viewed in terms of its longitudinal or cross-sectional data.

EXPERIMENTAL DESIGN

In an experimental design, the avowed purpose of the research is to answer a particular question. Generally, the question has to do with the effects of making a particular change or adjustment to a single variable. Experimental design research is the best way to diagnose causal relationships between variables. The independent variable is the factor manipulated by researchers, while the dependent variable is not adjusted intentionally. Experimental design research produces clear and easy-to-assess findings, but is perhaps more limited in its scope than other forms of research.

LIMITATIONS

One problem with experimental design is that certain variables, such as age, socioeconomic background, and health, are inextricable from the behavior of the subject but cannot be adjusted by the researcher. These are known as extraneous variables, and they can have a great deal of influence on the results of experimental research. Another potential problem with experimental design is that it can be hazardous or unethical; some questions or inquiries are seen as offensive by certain ethnic groups. Some researchers claim that there is a clear observation bias in experimental research. In other words, subjects perform differently in the context of an experiment than they would in real life. Also, experiments can be extremely expensive and time-intensive.

LONGITUDINAL DESIGN

Longitudinal design requires that subjects be monitored over an extremely long interval, often their entire lives. For instance, subjects of a longitudinal study may be interviewed every ten years. These experiments can be very difficult to develop and maintain, but they yield results that are unobtainable by any other method. Longitudinal studies can show lifelong progress, and can deliver fascinating insights about health, personal development, and social relationships over the long term. In order to get a full picture of human development, psychologists must continue to produce longitudinal studies.

DISADVANTAGES

Longitudinal studies have significant design flaws, not the least of which is the fact that the members of the subject group will change markedly over such a long interval. In some cases, the members of the group will move far away or die, making it difficult to keep up with them. Sometimes, the members of a longitudinal study will lose interest or decide they no longer want to participate, which leaves researchers with a great deal of wasted time and energy. Similarly, there can be changes in motivation and competence among the researchers; it is unlikely that the same group of scientists will administer the study from beginning to end. Some longitudinal studies run into funding problems, while others discover partway through that there are significant flaws in the methods or content of questioning. It is very difficult to make positive adjustments to a longitudinal study once it has begun.

DESCRIPTIVE RESEARCH

Descriptive research is a bit more free-form than experimental research; it entails the observation and recording of behavior. Descriptive research works best when it is aimed at identifying the instances of a particular action or type of action, such as aggressive behavior. Information for descriptive research can be obtained through observation, standardized tests, interviews, surveys, or case studies. In this type of research, the observer does not influence the behavior of the subject in any way. In other words, there is no manipulated variable. Descriptive research is not concerned with the causes of behavior, but simply with recording its appearances.

SOCIAL SURVEY

Social survey method of data collection, researchers take a look at the beliefs and behaviors of a large number of people. However, researchers do not individually question each member of the group. Instead, they draw a random sample of Representative members and question them. Information may be obtained from the sample group through face-to-face interviews, online questionnaires, or surveys sent through the mail. The results of social surveys can be valuable, so long as it can be assured that the responding group is representative of the population at large. Also, the survey instrument must have clear, comprehensible questions that produce easy to measure answers.

DISADVANTAGES

Social surveys must overcome internal biases and a lack of responses. The surveys depend on the voluntary participation of subjects, which is often not forthcoming. Moreover, there may be significant differences between those who respond to a survey and those who do not, and these differences can call into question the validity of the study. When social surveys gather information through interviews, it is quite possible that the subjects will adjust their responses depending on the personality and perceived interests of the researcher. In other words, the subject of an interview is likely to conform his answers to what he believes the researcher wants. Some people lie during interviews, and other people are unwilling to discuss personal matters candidly. Finally, social surveys are almost impossible to use with infants and young children.

NATURALISTIC OBSERVATION

Naturalistic observation is a technique for data collection in which researchers closely monitor the behavior of people in their normal, everyday environment. Perhaps the most common example of naturalistic observation occurs in schools, when administrators unobtrusively sit in on a class to observe teacher and student behavior. In some cases, the observer may record observations with a notepad, tape recorder, or video camera. It is important that the observer have access to basic information about the subjects, such as their ages and backgrounds. Typically, naturalistic observation is a part of descriptive research.

LIMITATIONS

Naturalistic observation tends to be only as good as the environment in which it is conducted. Since there is no manipulation of the environment, as there is in experimental research, all of the observations must be made with the caveat that total environmental control was not attempted. For this reason, there is always the possibility that unseen or unacknowledged factors are influencing behavior. Also, naturalistic observation tends to be weakened when the observer has specific biases or intentions in observation. Sometimes, observers merely see what they want to see. Finally, the subjects of naturalistic observation may alter their behavior because they know they are being observed.

CROSS-CULTURAL STUDIES

Cross-cultural studies are used to determine the validity of theories for more than one society. Sometimes, things that are true of one society are not true of another. The range of influences and cultural artifacts in one setting may vastly alter behavior and beliefs. To determine whether theories about one culture can be applied to another, researchers isolate a particular variable in two cultures and compare its appearances. For instance, in Hispanic culture there is often more loyalty to the matriarch than the patriarch. This has specific effects on child psychology, which can be studied and then compared with observations from other cultures.

LIMITATIONS

Cross-cultural studies require money and travel, so it is common for much of the data to be collected by amateurs and untrained researchers. This means that the quality of the data is variable. In some cultures, there may be very little background information, and so researchers must basically start from scratch. Cross-cultural studies often over-generalize about foreign cultures, ignoring the differences between individual members of the group. Also, researchers who conduct cross-cultural studies must guard against overemphasizing their own cultural perspective. For instance, it has long been a contention of third-world citizens that their lives are seen only through the lens of American and Western European thought.

STANDARDIZED TESTS IN DEVELOPMENTAL RESEARCH

Developmental researchers often use standardized tests, which are assessments with established questions and procedures for administration. Standardized tests are valuable because they can be replicated with different people and in different settings. At this point, the most effective standardized tests are those used to assess intelligence and personality. Of course, no standardized test is able to account for fluctuations in mood and motivation by the test-taker. Human behavior is unstable and inconsistent, which can weaken the validity of standardized testing.

POPULATION AND SAMPLE

In the context of research, a population is the whole group being studied. Typically, the size of the population will be defined by the parameters of the study. The population could be the citizens of a town, the members of a high school class, or the attendees of a certain church. However large or small, the population must be strictly defined in order for the research to be useful. Sometimes, it is impractical for an entire population to be studied, and so researchers will select a representative portion of the population, known as a sample. Samples can be chosen at random, but it is better for researchers to use established method of sampling. It is very important that the method of sampling be capable of extracting a representative selection of people.

TIME SAMPLING AND EVENT SAMPLING

Time sampling and event sampling are techniques by which an observer can guarantee objectivity in naturalistic studies. These are methods of assuring symmetry in observation. In time sampling, the observer selects a particular interval, and then counts the instances of the target behavior during that interval. For example, the observer might decide to count instances over ten minute spans for each of the subjects. In event sampling, the observer reports the duration of each instance of the target behavior. Every time the behavior occurs, the observer uses a clock or stopwatch to measure how long it goes on.

COHORT EFFECTS

All of the influences on the development of a person that have to do with the era in which he lives are known as cohort effects. For example, children of the Great Depression are likely to exhibit different behaviors towards money and financial responsibility than are children of the 1990s, a period of relative prosperity. The mores and attitudes of a society change over time, and the citizens of the population are likely to receive different opportunities and messages from the community depending on when they were born. Researchers must pay particular attention to cohort effects when examining the effects of age on subjects; sometimes, what is believed to be an idiosyncrasy or a personality characteristic is actually a response to environmental stimuli.

ETHICS IN DEVELOPMENTAL RESEARCH

Gathering data about people may be the primary intention of researchers, but it is also necessary to guard the rights and privacy of subjects. The subject of a research project should never run the risk of physical or mental harm. For this reason, university-funded or -operated projects typically have to be approved by an ethics committee, and professional organizations like the American Psychological Association and Society for Research in Child Development have strict guidelines for research in their fields. There are requirements for consent and confidentiality. The subjects of a research study must be given sufficient information about the purpose of the study and the methods to be used.

CONFIDENTIALITY IN RESEARCH

All those people who participate in a study have a right to privacy and confidentiality. In most studies, the data is recorded and reported in such a way that it is impossible to ascertain the identity of the subject. Also, the information collected by the researcher should remain confidential as much as possible. The only scenario in which a researcher has the right to divulge confidential information is if it has the potential to affect the safety of the subject or others. In order to divulge specific information related to individual performance, the researcher needs to obtain permission from the subject.

INFORMED CONSENT AND DECEPTION IN RESEARCH

In research, subjects have the right to be told about the purpose, methodology, and potential risks of participation. There are established requirements related to informed consent, meaning that participants have the right to obtain whatever information they want before they assent. Also, subjects have the right to end their participation at any time. Of course, in some situations the research will be invalidated if the participants are fully informed ahead of time. When this is the case, it is the responsibility of the researcher to ensure that this deception will not harm the participants, and that all of the information justifying this deception is made available to participants upon completion of the study.

Biological Development Throughout the Life Span

GENES AND CHROMOSOMES

The fundamental unit of heredity is the gene, a tiny part of the cell that communicates information about development to the body. Genes are passed on from parent to child. A gene is a short part of the DNA molecule found in the nucleus of every cell. Among the functions stimulated by genes are cell reproduction and protein synthesis. Chromosomes, meanwhile, are tiny, thread-like structures composed of DNA and found in the nuclei of cells. A human fetus has 23 pairs, composed in equal parts of genetic material from the mother and father.

> **Review Video: Chromosomes**
> Visit mometrix.com/academy and enter code: 132083

DOMINANT AND RECESSIVE GENES

Human beings inherit genes from each parent for certain characteristics. For instance, a baby will have the genes related to hair color from both his mother and his father. When one of the genes is dominant, it overpowers the other gene and manifests in the child's development. The gene that is overpowered is called the recessive gene. Recessive genes may contribute to development if they are reinforced by another recessive gene in the same pair. However, if the child has one recessive gene and one dominant gene in a particular chromosome, the dominant gene will always win out.

GENETIC COUNSELING

When an individual or a couple discovers a family history of genetic disease or abnormality, they may consult with a genetic counselor to determine the likelihood of passing this condition on to their offspring. Many people do not want to have a child if they feel there is a strong likelihood that the child will be severely handicapped. In addition, it can be very expensive and time-consuming to care for a handicapped child. A genetic counselor can provide information to couples so that they can make a more educated decision about reproduction. Sometimes, genetic counselors are asked to consult with couples who do not have particular genetic disorders in their history, but are simply advanced in age.

CHROMOSOMAL ABNORMALITIES

When a human being has too many or too few chromosomes, he may display particular tendencies. For instance, if a person has an extra chromosome 21, he will have Down syndrome, which manifests as physical deformity and intellectual disabilities. Males with an extra X chromosome have Klinefelter's syndrome, which is linked to physical abnormalities. Females with a missing X chromosome have Turner syndrome, which manifests as intellectual disabilities, physical abnormalities, and shortness. Males with an extra Y chromosome have XYY syndrome, which tends to make them exceptionally tall.

GENE-LINKED ABNORMALITIES

There are more than 7000 diseases and abnormalities that are thought to be caused by genetic issues. These conditions range in severity. For instance, many African-Americans suffer from sickle-cell anemia, a blood disorder that prevents the effective distribution of oxygen. Genetic abnormalities are also to blame for diabetes, in which the body produces insufficient insulin and has a hard time regulating blood-sugar levels. Another genetic abnormality is tied to cystic fibrosis, which causes glandular malfunction, digestive problems, and clogged respiratory passageways. A classic genetic abnormality is hemophilia, in which blood fails to clot properly. If left untreated, hemophilia can be fatal. Other common genetic abnormalities include Huntington's disease, Tay-Sachs disease, spina bifida, and phenylketonuria.

Divisions of the Prenatal Period

Biologists isolate three divisions in the prenatal period of infant development: the germinal period, the embryonic period, and the fetal period. The germinal period, which consists of the first two weeks after conception, is initiated by the fertilization of the egg and concludes with the zygote affixing itself to the uterine wall. During the embryonic period, which lasts from the end of the germinal period to about the eighth week of pregnancy, the major organs begin to develop and the body takes on a recognizably human appearance. In the final period, the fetal, the body becomes viable. The fetal period runs from about the ninth week until the end of the pregnancy.

Prenatal Development
Germinal Period

The germinal period of pregnancy lasts for two weeks after fertilization. In the first week, the zygote moves from the fallopian tubes into the uterus and attaches to the wall there. At this point, cell division through mitosis has already begun. In mitosis, a cell splits apart into two other cells with the same chromosomes and genes as the original cell. At the end of the germinal period, there will be enough cells for the inner cell mass of the blastocyst to have three distinct layers proceeding from outside to inside: the ectoderm, which will become the sense organs, skin, and nervous system; the mesoderm which will become the circulatory system, bones, kidneys, and muscles; and the endoderm, which will become the bladder, respiratory system, digestive system, and part of the reproductive system.

Embryonic Period

During the embryonic period, it becomes possible to see that the embryo is a human fetus. The embryonic period runs from the third to the eighth week of pregnancy. At this point, both cephalocaudal and proximodistal development are in full swing. Cephalocaudal development begins in the head and moves down through the body, while proximodistal development is the growth of tissue on the left and right sides of what is known as the primitive streak, the early stages of spinal cord development.

Fetal Period

The final period of prenatal development, known as the fetal period, extends from about the ninth week of pregnancy to birth. The embryo is now known as a fetus, with a face, internal organs, and appendages. The fetus will even have fingers and toes. After about 20 weeks of gestation, the fetus will be approximately one foot long and will have a heartbeat that can be heard with a stethoscope. Four or five weeks later, the fetus will be sufficiently developed to survive outside the womb, though it is likely that such an early baby would require respiratory assistance.

Teratogen

A teratogen is a material or action that can adversely affect the development of a fetus. Teratogens can be responsible for miscarriages and birth defects, as well as more minor problems. Maternal disease, advanced age, exposure to hazardous materials, and nicotine are all teratogens. In addition, caffeine, alcohol, blood disorders, unhealthy foods, and a lack of prenatal care all have the potential to be teratogens. Many drugs, both prescription and over-the-counter, are teratogens.

NATURAL CHILDBIRTH

Natural childbirth methods aim to avoid medication during labor by teaching the mother breathing and relaxation techniques. In a natural childbirth, the mother is wide awake and in full control of her senses. She does not receive any medication to accelerate or anesthetize labor. Although the emphasis is on the role of the mother, there are duties for both parents and assistants in natural childbirth. In some cases, of course, it will simply be impossible for the mother to endure labor without medication.

STAGES OF BIRTH

Doctors usually distinguish three stages in the birth process: labor, delivery, and afterbirth. Labor can last 12 or more hours, and is often initiated by the rupture of the amniotic sac. During labor, the woman endures painful contractions about one minute long and occurring every 15 to 20 minutes. These contractions stimulate the dilation of the cervix and the movement of the fetus towards the vagina. In the second stage of birth, delivery, the head of the baby moves through the cervix into the vagina. At this point, however, the umbilical cord still connects the baby to the mother. In the final stage, afterbirth, the placenta and umbilical cord follow the baby through the mother's vagina and out.

MEDICATIONS USED IN CHILDBIRTH

There are three categories of medication used during childbirth: analgesics, anesthesia, and oxytocics. Analgesics reduce pain, and include such drug types as tranquilizers, narcotics, and barbiturates. Anesthesia, on the other hand, entirely negates sensation in a particular part of the body. A general anesthetic renders the mother entirely unconscious. For instance, many women receive an epidural block during labor, which numbs their body below the waist. It is not recommended to use general anesthesia during labor. Finally, oxytocics stimulate contractions. Perhaps the most common of these is the synthetic hormone oxytocin, the advantages and disadvantages of which are not yet fully known.

APGAR SCORING SYSTEM

In 1953, Dr. Virginia Apgar developed a scoring system for assessing the physical condition of newborns. The Apgar tests should be performed one and five minutes after birth. The infant is assigned scores in five categories: pulse, skin color, reflexes, activity, and respiration. In each of these categories, the infant receives a zero, one, or two, depending on positive or negative characteristics. If the total score is three or less, the infant needs immediate medical attention. Infants who score from four to seven possibly need assistance, while infants who score seven or above are considered to be viable and in need of no assistance.

MIDWIVES AND DOULAS

Despite being uncommon in the United States, midwives assist in more births than doctors worldwide. In the United States, midwives only attend at about 10% of births. In order to become a certified nurse midwife, a person must have a nursing degree, special training, and board certification. Around the country, there are midwives employed by birthing centers and hospitals. A doula, on the other hand, provides more palliative assistance to the woman during childbirth. Doulas may have licensure and professional affiliation, but this is not a necessity. For the most part, doulas just provide emotional support, information, and physical assistance to the laboring woman.

BENEFITS OF BREAST FEEDING

The precise benefits of breast-feeding have not been demonstrated by experiment, but there appear to be strong correlations between the practice and mother-child bonding. In addition, breast-feeding mothers are less likely to develop breast and ovarian cancer and type-2 diabetes. Children who breast-feed have a lower incidence of sudden infant death syndrome, the skin inflammation atopic dermatitis, middle ear infection, gastrointestinal infections, lower respiratory infections, obesity, and type-1 diabetes. Again, however, all of these findings are correlational rather than experimental; conclusive research on the advantages of breast-feeding versus bottlefeeding has yet to be performed.

SIDS

Sudden infant death syndrome, known commonly as SIDS, is a mystifying and tragic cause of newborn mortality. It occurs when an infant stops breathing and dies, for no immediately discernible reason. Although the precise cause of sudden infant death syndrome is not known, the following have been identified as risk factors: abnormal brainstem function, sleep apnea, exposure to tobacco smoke, low birth weight, low socioeconomic status, African-American or Inuit ethnicity, family history of SIDS, and excessively soft mattresses. In addition, research suggests that children who sleep with a pacifier are less likely to have SIDS.

IMMUNIZATION

These days, individuals in developed countries receive many immunizations against diseases that can threaten health and life. Vaccines stimulate the body to produce a certain kind of antibody, so that the body will be ready should it be attacked by a certain kind of virus. The Centers for Disease Control recommends childhood immunization against polio, rubella, measles, mumps, chickenpox, meningitis, diphtheria, tetanus, and whooping cough. Many doctors also recommend a childhood immunization against hepatitis B. This immunization may be administered almost immediately after birth. Some vaccines must be administered several times. In the United States, it is common for schools and child care facilities to require certain immunizations.

FOOD PYRAMID

The United States Department of Agriculture created the food pyramid to illustrate the composition of a healthy diet. On the food pyramid, foods are arranged into four levels, depending on the volume in which they should be consumed. Grains are on the bottom level. Included in this category are bread, rice, pasta, and cereal. On the second level are fruits and vegetables. This means that a person should consume slightly more grains than fruits or vegetables. Above the fruits and vegetables are two groups, the meats and the dairy. Meats include eggs, nuts, fish, and dry beans. The dairy group includes cheese, milk, and yogurt. The top of the pyramid is made up of fats, oils, and sweets. The tip of the pyramid is very small, indicating that a person should not consume very many foods from this category.

OBESITY

In simple terms, a person puts on weight when he consumes more calories than he burns. It is easier to overconsume when eating foods high in fat and sugar, since these foods contain more calories than do fruits and vegetables. In the United States, many individuals develop poor dietary habits during childhood, and these habits contribute to the development of obesity later in life. A sedentary lifestyle, with a great deal of time in front of a computer or television screen, often leads to obesity. Of course, many people have a hereditary disposition towards obesity, and may have to strive throughout life to overcome this genetic inclination. Also, research has suggested that low socioeconomic status is correlated with obesity.

MALNUTRITION

A person can develop malnutrition if he eats a bad diet or has a physiological inability to absorb and use certain nutrients. Interestingly, doctors also define overconsumption of food as malnutrition.

In other words, an obese person can be as poorly nourished as an emaciated person. Malnutrition can be caused by a general lack of calories, or a specific lack of protein, vitamins, or minerals. Epidemics of malnutrition are often related to natural disasters, war, and extremely bad economic conditions. Moreover, individuals who know very little about nutrition are more likely to become malnourished. Some of the diseases related to malnutrition and include anemia, caused by low levels of iron or copper; kwashiorkor, associated with low levels of protein; and marasmus, associated with the general low calorie consumption.

GROSS VS. FINE MOTOR SKILLS

Physiologists make a distinction between gross motor skills, which require large muscle groups, and fine motor skills, which require the use of small muscle groups, like those on the fingers and hands. Some examples of gross motor skills are standing, kicking, walking, running, crawling, and throwing. Fine motor skills are exemplified by actions like typing, sewing, sign language, and drawing. It takes a person much longer to develop fine motor skills than gross motor skills. Many of the important day-to-day activities require fine motor skills, however. For instance, putting on clothes and tying shoes require intricate movements by the fingers. Of course, most activities require a combination of fine and gross motor skills.

MOTOR SKILL DEVELOPMENT

TWO-YEAR OLDS

The second year after birth is marked by rapid progress in motor skills. In the 15th month after birth, a child will often be able to walk by himself. By the end of the 24th month, that same child will be able to run and jump forward about one foot in distance. A two-year-old should be able to drag a toy, walk backwards, kick and throw a ball, and balance in a squatting position. The child at this age should be able to ascend and descend stairs on his hands and knees. The two-year-old should be able to turn the pages in a book, hold a plastic cup, and stack blocks.

AGES THREE TO FIVE

At three years of age, a child should be able to catch a ball, run, jump, hop, and ride a tricycle or big wheel. At this point, fine motor skills will have developed as well, and the child should be able to draw a reasonably straight line and copy a circle. By the age of four years, the child should be able to gallop, put on clothes, and navigate complicated play equipment, like a jungle gym. As for fine motor skills, a four-year-old should be able to cut with scissors and replicate letters and numbers on paper. At five years, the child should be able to hop on one foot, sprint, and skip. A five-year-old should be able to copy all the basic symbols and shapes.

MIDDLE CHILDHOOD YEARS

Entering middle childhood, the rate of motor skill development slows down. Middle childhood, which runs from about five to fourteen years of age, is marked by the gradual refinement of basic gross and fine motor skills. During these years, the child will become more coordinated and in control of his body. A child at this age should be able to learn games like baseball and basketball, and should be able to master riding a bike or a skateboard. During middle childhood, endurance and intensity of effort increase, and there are significantly fewer differences between boys and girls then there will be later in life.

LEARNING TO WALK

It is typical for a child in the United States to begin walking between 11 and 15 months after birth. The development of walking requires a number of fundamental gross motor skills, like raising the head, rolling over, and sitting without support. The muscles of the legs and torso must be sufficiently developed to hold the child upright. A child typically begins to walk by pulling herself up into a standing position, and then walking with some assistance. For many children, the process starts with crawling, then creeping, and finally standing upright before walking. However, some children skip one of these steps. Walking requires enough strength to balance on one leg briefly while stepping forward with the other.

DEVELOPMENT OF MANUAL SKILLS

Two months after birth, an infant will be able to move his arms and upper body toward an object, but he will not be able to clutch it. Three months after birth, the infant will be able to incorporate shoulder and elbow into his movement, though he still will be swiping with a closed fist. A month later, the child will be able to use an open hand to grasp an object, and approximately five months after birth, the child will be able to gently touch the object. There may be some semblance of a grip at this stage, though for most children a recognizable grip does not develop until about 36 weeks after birth. At first, a child is likely to put objects into his mouth. After about two years of development, infants should be able to hold and use a writing utensil, a fork or spoon, and a toothbrush.

SEXUAL DEVELOPMENT

TESTOSTERONE

Testosterone is a sex hormone produced in both sexes by the adrenal glands, as well as in male testicles and female ovaries. Testosterone is an androgen, and is deeply involved in the changes that take place during puberty. Testosterone stimulates the male body to increase muscle mass, deepen the voice, and produce facial hair. Testosterone also motivates the sex drive and the production of sperm. The diminution of testosterone production is responsible for the slackening of the sex drive later in life. Synthetic testosterone is found in anabolic steroids, dangerous drugs taken improve strength and athletic performance.

ESTROGENS

The ovaries produce a set of hormones called estrogens, of which the most prominent is estradiol. These hormones stimulate many of the changes in the female body during puberty. For instance, estrogen is responsible for the thickening of the uterine lining, and thus for the initiation of menstruation. Both males and females produce small amounts of estrogen in their fat tissues. Males also produce a small amount of estrogen in their testes. Doctors do not yet understand the function of estrogen in the male body. In middle age, a woman will begin to produce less estrogen, and eventually she will not produce enough to stimulate menstruation. At this point, a woman is said to have reached menopause.

ADOLESCENT SEXUAL ATTITUDES AND BEHAVIORS

In adolescence, people receive influence on moral issues from a number of different sources. Although parental values are still important, the adolescent also derives much of his feeling about morality from religious sources and teachers. Sometimes, the values of the parents or community are seen as stifling by the adolescent, who then rebels against them. Teenagers are likely to imitate the behavior of their family members, and so youngsters with an older and sexually active sibling, a single parent, or a mother who became sexually active at a young age tend to be more promiscuous. Poor, crowded, crime-ridden, and segregated neighborhoods have higher rates of teenage sexual activity. Most psychologists also feel that the media, and especially television, contribute to a climate of permissiveness.

ADOLESCENT SEXUAL IDENTITY

Adolescents are engaged in the turbulent process of developing a sexual identity, a process made necessary and more complicated by the rapid increase in sex hormones. It is imperative for adolescents to manage their behavior appropriately, so as to avoid pregnancy and sexually transmitted diseases. Some adolescents find that their sexual attractions are centered on people of the same sex or members of both sexes. When this is the case, the adolescent is likely to have more trouble establishing sexual identity. Developing a sexual identity is even more problematic for transgender teenagers.

Sexual orientation

A person's sexual orientation is how he interacts with other people sexually, emotionally, and romantically. The three major sexual orientations are heterosexual, homosexual, and bisexual. Sexual orientation does not necessarily manifest in overt behavior; it may be simply a person's fantasies and thoughts. Nevertheless, sexual orientation is a huge component of self-conception. A number of physiological and environmental factors contribute to sexual orientation. Indeed, the mixture of hormones received by the fetus before birth may have an impact on sexual orientation. The extent to which a person considers or acknowledges his sexual orientation is extremely variable. Some people do not fully acknowledge their sexual orientation until adulthood. For the most part, though, it is believed that sexual orientation is fixed and permanent.

Homosexual and bisexual

Homosexual means having a sexual interest in members of the same sex. A person is considered a homosexual even if they never engage in homosexual actions, so long as they have sexual and romantic thoughts and fantasies about members of the same sex. Male homosexuals are often referred to as gay, while female homosexuals are called lesbians.

Bisexual is having sexual and romantic interest in both males and females. Again, a person does not have to act on bisexual desires in order to be classified as a bisexual. More so than heterosexuality or homosexuality, bisexuality is believed to fluctuate over the course of a life.

Transgender persons and transvestic disorder

Transgender persons are people who feel at odds from their anatomical sex. In other words, people whose felt gender identity is distinct from their physically perceived or societal gender. In the past, transgender persons had only the option of wearing the clothing and assuming the lifestyle of the opposite sex. Now, transgender persons can receive hormone therapy and surgery to give their bodies the desired characteristics. Biological men are more likely than biological women to be transgender. Transvestic disorder is a type of paraphilia wherein one receives recurrent pleasure from dressing in the clothes associated with the opposite sex. This is much more common among biological men, particularly heterosexuals.

Sexuality in older adults

Because of declining levels of sex hormones, interest in sexual activity tends to decrease in late adulthood. Some adults, in particular men, experience problems with arousal. Also, middle-aged and elderly men and women are less likely to have a regular sexual partner. Health problems and a lack of general mobility can diminish interest in sex. Nevertheless, in 2007 a study of 3000 adults between the ages of 57 and 85 reported that a significant number were sexually active.

Cephalocaudal and proximodistal principles of development

Human physical development can be described as occurring according to either the cephalocaudal or proximodistal principles. In the cephalocaudal model, human development starts in the head, and specifically the brain, and moves down through the torso into the lower extremities. This model aligns with the development of the fetus and young child. In particular, the nervous system's development seems to begin with the brain stem and proceed downward. The proximodistal model, on the other hand, describes growth as progressing from a central axis, the spinal column, outward to the extremities. This model of growth is consistent with the superiority of strength in the core of the body, and the necessity of developing central muscular systems before peripheral ones.

Brain

There are three main structures in the brain: the cerebrum, the cerebellum, and the brain stem. The cerebrum makes up about 85% of the brain's weight, and is divided into left and right hemispheres. Each of these hemispheres has four lobes: frontal, occipital, temporal, and parietal. The frontal lobes control processes like cognition, intentional motion, and planning. The occipital lobes are mainly concerned with vision. The temporal lobes manage functions like audition, language production, and memory. The parietal lobes are related to motor functions, spatial orientation, and concentration. The cerebellum is mainly devoted to posture, physical orientation, and balance. Finally, the brainstem controls the most basic functions of the body, like breathing and circulation.

Nervous system

The nervous system controls the functions of the body, and collects information about body processes. It has a few components. The central nervous system consists of the brain and spinal cord. The central nervous system compiles information about the external and internal environment and generates responses to these stimuli. The information acted upon by the central nervous system is collected by the peripheral nervous system. Information is transmitted to the spinal cord and brain through 12 pairs of cranial nerves and 31 pairs of spinal nerves. All of the body functions that are not under conscious control, as for instance respiration and digestion, are controlled by the autonomic nervous system.

Brain development

Prenatal

About 2 ½ weeks after fertilization, the brain and central nervous system of the infant begin to develop. The first step is the emergence of a neural tube, which is a long, hollow structure along the dorsal side of the embryo. The top of this tube closes off about 25 days after conception, and the lower end closes off two days later. At the top end of the tube, a brain will develop. About five weeks after fertilization, nerve cells, also known as neurons, will begin to proliferate. Approximately 23 weeks into the pregnancy, connections between these neurons will be formed.

Early childhood

During the first years of childhood, the nervous system and brain develop rapidly. In part, this is because the infant is experiencing a wealth of novel sensations. As the brain and nervous system develop, there are more connections between axons and dendrites, and there is additional myelin on the outside of axons. In other words, the synaptic connections in the brain and nervous system are faster and more numerous. Also, in early childhood the brain gets better at communicating with itself. There is particular progress made in the frontal cortex, which is associated with higher-level functions like planning and problem-solving. Amazingly, a five-year-old will have already obtained approximately 90% of his adult brain weight.

Middle childhood

In middle childhood, the brain and nervous system continue to develop properly, so long as the child receives sufficient sleep and nutrition. However, malnutrition, a lack of sensory stimulation, abuse, or a dangerous home life can impede the progress of development. During middle childhood, as the child passes through elementary school, his cognition will improve in terms of speed, volume, and efficiency. Memory makes significant progress during this period, and the child develops the ability to reason abstractly and solve complicated problems.

BRAIN FUNCTION

MIDLIFE

In midlife, or between the ages of 45 and 65, the brain and nervous system begin to slow a bit. People at this age will have more crystallized, or permanent knowledge, but will have less intellectual agility and deftness. It may take a person in this stage of life a bit longer to solve a new problem. Nevertheless, a person in midlife will have more experience dealing with different situations, and will be able to apply knowledge more broadly. During midlife, the memory may begin to diminish, as the prefrontal cortex atrophies. However, people who remain intellectually active tend to lose fewer brain cells.

OLDER ADULTS

Over the span from age 20 to 90, a person will lose between 5 and 10% of brain weight. Moreover, the brain will decrease during this interval by 15% in volume. Some scientists believe that this decrease is caused by the elimination of dendrites, damage to the myelin sheaths on axons, or to the deaths of brain cells. However, none of these theories have been conclusively proved. As the brain shrinks, the individual will experience memory and cognitive deficits. Also, older adults tend to have diminished reflexes and physical coordination.

SENSORY PERCEPTION OF AN INFANT

Recent advances in technology and research methods have given scientists the ability to ascertain the sensory information available to infants. For instance, scientists now know that newborns possess all five senses, though the function of the senses may be primitive. The hearing of an infant is very good, but the vision is poor, because the optic nerve and retina are still in incipient phases. Sense of hearing seems to be operational even in the last two or three months of gestation. Anyone who has seen an infant receive a shot knows that he can feel pain, and other experiments have determined that infants react differently to various tastes and smells.

DEVELOPMENT OF VISION IN AN INFANT

When an infant is born, he has an unfinished optic nerve, lens, and ocular muscles. The result is that the vision of a newborn is imperfect. For instance, an infant sees an object 20 feet away about as vividly as an adult sees an object 40 feet away. After six months out of the womb, and infant's vision has improved to the point that he can see a object 20 feet away about as well as an adult sees an object 40 feet away. Eight months after birth, an infant's vision is as good as adult vision. Babies typically develop the ability to focus between two and three months after birth.

DEVELOPMENT OF HEARING IN INFANTS

It has been determined that the sense of hearing is well-established even during the last two or three months of pregnancy. At this point, a fetus is able to hear music and the mother's voice. In the months after birth, the infant becomes better at noticing differences in the loudness, pitch, and location of sound. Newborns tend to distinguish loud sounds better than soft ones, and high-pitched sounds better than low-pitched sounds. By two years of age, infants can hear low-pitched sounds quite well. Also, by this point the infant will be very good at determining the origin of sounds.

SENSE OF TOUCH IN YOUNG CHILDREN

Newborn children are capable of distinguishing differences in temperature, though they do not seem to mind small variations. Newborns are extremely sensitive to touch, and often respond with reflexive actions. For instance, if an infant is touched on the lip, he will automatically suck. If the child is touched on the side of the head, he will naturally turn in the direction of the touch. This is known as the rooting reflex. The development of the tactile sense helps to develop the sense of sight, as children use their eyes and hands to explore the world. Children often get a great deal of pleasure from handling materials of different texture.

SENSE OF SMELL IN INFANCY

Infants are born with a sense of smell. They prefer some odors to others, and react in proportion to the strength of the smell. In particular, research suggests that infants like familiar odors, like that of their mother. Also, infants have been found to prefer pleasing smells, like vanilla, and to dislike smells like garbage. Infants who breast-feed seem to like the smell of the breast milk. An infant will indicate his opinion about a smell by turning his head towards the origin, or by making a face.

SENSE OF TASTE IN INFANCY

From birth, people have a sense of taste. An infant indicates his preferences by sucking and making faces. Infants who are given a sweet liquid tend to suck more slowly, almost as if they want to prolong the pleasure of the taste. An infant who is sucking a sweet liquid will appear to smile. An infant given a sour solution, on the other hand, will appear to grimace, and will often refuse to suck. Some babies dislike salty solutions, while others do not seem to care about saltiness one way or the other. A preference for salty foods seems to develop after about four months.

PUBERTY

Puberty is the set of physical changes that shift a person from childhood into adulthood. The age at which a person begins puberty varies widely. Girls tend to enter puberty before boys. A girl may begin to develop breasts and pubic hair at age 9, while a boy will not experience any genital growth until at least age 10. Menstruation typically begins around age 11 or 12 for girls, but it may occur as late as 15. For some people, puberty only lasts a year and a half, though it can last up to five years.

PHYSICAL CHANGES

One of the most immediately apparent changes caused by puberty is a rapid growth in height and weight. Girls typically begin this growth spurt about two years earlier than boys. In the midst of this growth spurt, however, a girl may grow 3 ½ inches each year, while a boy can grow up to 4 inches annually. During puberty, both boys and girls will begin to develop pubic and underarm hair. Girls will experience breast development, and will begin to menstruate. The first menstruation is called menarche. During puberty, the hips of the female will expand, while the male will develop more musculature and facial hair. Males will also experience a deepening of the voice.

ENDOCRINE SYSTEM

During puberty, the endocrine system will stimulate changes by producing a different cocktail of hormones. In particular, hormones associated with puberty are produced by the hypothalamus, gonads, and pituitary gland. The hypothalamus is located in the brain, where it manages the sympathetic nervous system, coordinates the nervous and endocrine systems, and maintains a steady body temperature (a process known as homeostasis). The pituitary gland monitors other glands and regulates the overall growth of the body. Gonads are often considered to be synonymous with the male testes, though the female ovaries are gonads as well. Gonads produce testosterone and estradiol, which is a form of estrogen directly linked with puberty.

> **Review Video: Endocrine System**
> Visit mometrix.com/academy and enter code: 678939

ADOLESCENT EGOCENTRISM

The psychologist David Elkind accepted Piaget's assertion regarding adolescent egocentrism, though he distinguished two characteristics, namely the personal fable and the imaginary audience. The personal fable is the adolescent's assumption that his problems are original and cannot be understood by other people. Sometimes, this can lead to problems, as the adolescent may become possessed by feelings of invulnerability and take unnecessary risks. The imaginary audience concept refers to the common supposition made by adolescents that other people are as interested in their problems as they are. Because of this perceived attention, the adolescent becomes excessively self-conscious, self-critical, or self-admiring.

EMERGING ADULTHOOD

Dr. Jeffrey Arnett, in a 2000 article in American Psychologist, defined emerging adulthood as a period of development between ages 18 and 29, during which a person focuses on developing their adult persona and choosing a career and lifestyle. Emerging adults have five characteristics in common. They are actively working to develop an identity, in part by finding a vocation. They live unstable lifestyles, frequently moving and changing jobs. They are primarily focused on themselves. They feel as if they are in between stages of life. Finally, emerging adults are generally optimistic about their future.

PHYSICAL PEAK OF PERFORMANCE

For most people, peak physical performance occurs between the ages of 20 and 30. A female reaches her maximum height at age 20, while a male may continue to grow until age 30. By the age of 35, both men and women will have achieved peak bone mass and muscular endurance. The heart and lungs seem to perform best during the 20s, after which point the body begins a slow decline. The tone and strength of muscle diminishes, fatty tissue increases, and the lens loses some ability to register focus and shade. Also, hearing begins to diminish around the age of 30.

HEALTH ISSUES OF EMERGING AND EARLY ADULTHOOD

Emerging adults tend to be quite healthy, but they may be developing habits of behavior that will cause problems later in life. For instance, many emerging adults smoke, drink too much, sleep too little, exercise infrequently, and eat bad foods. Also, emerging adults may not take care of their reproductive health, and may not have access to basic health care services. Substance addiction and sexually transmitted diseases are especially common among emerging adults. Interestingly, according to the Berkeley Longitudinal Study, a strong predictor of life satisfaction at age 70 is when an individual at age 30 receives help to overcome these health issues.

MIDDLE ADULTHOOD

The precise range of middle adulthood is disputed. Although the numerical midpoint of life is about 39, most Americans consider middle age or middle adulthood to be between 40 and 65. During middle age, a body begins to lose some of its efficiency, and the sensory organs decline in function. Men tend to endure more significant drop-offs than women, and indeed more men die during middle age than do women. In particular, people with African ancestry seem to be prone to significant health problems during middle age.

Physical Changes Common in Middle Adulthood

In middle adulthood, most people undergo subtle but significant physical changes. The skin will begin to wrinkle, sag, and may develop some age spots. The hair will turn gray and become thinner. Many men go bald during middle adulthood. Height will diminish slightly, and weight is likely to increase. In particular, middle-aged people tend to put on fat. At the same time, people over the age of 50 lose muscle tone, and thereby strength. This is particularly true in the legs and the back. Around this time, the tendons of the ligaments lose their elasticity, and the person is more likely to suffer from joint stiffness. Women are susceptible to osteoporosis during middle adulthood, and both men and women must be on the lookout for high blood pressure, arthritis, and diabetes.

Cholesterol

High cholesterol and high blood pressure, otherwise known as hypertension, are problems often faced by middle-aged adults. There are two kinds of cholesterol: high-density lipoprotein (HDL, also known as good cholesterol) and low-density lipoprotein (LDL, also known as bad cholesterol). Some cholesterol is necessary, but if there is too much low-density lipoprotein in the bloodstream, it can build up the on the walls of the arteries and cause hardening, a condition known as atherosclerosis. Individuals with elevated levels of high-density lipoprotein and low levels of low-density lipoprotein have a reduced risk of cardiovascular disease.

Presbyopia

Presbyopia is an aging-related eye condition in which the lens hardens and the eye loses the ability to focus closely. This condition typically sets in around age 40. A person who suffers from presbyopia is likely to have a hard time reading small print or working on a computer. He is likely to prefer reading type from a distance of several feet. Bifocals, contact lenses, or half-glasses can be used to improve the vision. Also, some people afflicted with presbyopia benefit from surgically implanted lenses or laser correction surgery.

Vision Changes in Late Adulthood

In late adulthood, almost all aspects of vision decline. The peripheral vision becomes smaller, as there is a general decrease in the span of the visual field. The eye becomes less adaptable to variations in light, and many people find it difficult to drive or walk at night as they grow older. Depth perception and color differentiation both diminish with age. Moreover, people are more likely to be afflicted by eye problems like glaucoma, cataracts, and macular degeneration as they age.

Effects of Aging on Hearing

Around age 30, people begin to experience diminished hearing. In particular, it becomes difficult for people to hear high-pitched sounds. At the age of 50, about a third of all men and a quarter of all women will be unable to understand a whisper. The degradation of hearing ability can be accelerated by prolonged exposure to loud noises, and so people who operate heavy equipment or work near loud machinery are more likely to suffer declines. By the age of 70, about 10% of the population will experience significant hearing loss, and by the age of 84 about 20% will have very poor hearing.

Menopause and Perimenopause

Menopause: The point in a woman's life when menstruation ceases entirely. Most women undergo menopause in their 40s or 50s. During menopause, a woman is likely to endure side-effects of reduced estrogen production, like fatigue, hot flashes, and disturbances in sleep. However, some women experience no symptoms of menopause.

Perimenopause: A period of declining intensity and volume in menstruation. Perimenopause can last a decade, and may be marked by depression, heart palpitations, and headaches.

THEORIES OF AGING

CELLULAR CLOCK THEORY

This theory, developed by Leonard Hayflick in 1977, asserts that a cell can only divide 75 or 80 times at the most. Moreover, an older person's cells will be able to divide fewer times. This cellular clock places restrictions on the age to which a human being can live, which, for Hayflick, was about 125 years. Since the advancement of the cellular clock theory, scientists have begun to focus on the reasons for cell death. One theory is that cells die because the DNA sequences at the end of each chromosome, also known as telomeres, become shorter every time the cell divides. Eventually, the telomeres are so short that the cell can no longer reproduce.

BIOLOGICAL THEORIES

There are a few different biological theories for aging. According to the wear-and-tear theory advanced by rheumatologist James Fries, the human body is simply destined to fall apart due to frailty after about 85 years. Another theory, called the error accumulation theory, asserts that human beings die because cells in their bodies accumulate errors when duplicating. According to the free-radical or accumulation-of-metabolic-wastes theory, the body builds up metabolic waste, and especially free radicals, which are damaging and ultimately fatal to the molecules of the body.

LEADING CAUSES OF DEATH

The leading causes of death among infants are related to birth defects and under-development. Infants may die in a miscarriage before birth, may be stillborn, or may die during the birthing process. Among children, most deaths are caused by illness or accidents, in particular drowning, poisoning, and car crashes. The illnesses that most often afflict children are heart disease and cancer. The leading causes of death among adolescents are murder, automobile accidents, and suicide. The leading causes of death among young adults and middle-aged adults are accidents, cancer, and heart disease. Among older adults, chronic disease is the most common cause of death, and it is typically preceded by a prolonged period of disability.

KUBLER-ROSS'S STAGES OF DYING

Elisabeth Kubler-Ross in 1969 outlined five stages through which a person passes during the dying process. In the first stage, denial and isolation, the person has not yet accepted the reality of impending death. In the second stage, anger, the person rages against his circumstances and blames God or others. The third stage, bargaining, is marked by attempts to compromise or make a deal to prolong life. During the fourth stage, depression, the person begins to accept the reality of impending death and may become withdrawn. During stage five, acceptance, the person acknowledges the inevitability of his death, and reaches a sort of peace.

CRITICISMS

The five stages of death outlined by Kubler-Ross have been criticized heavily since being issued in 1969. According to Robert Kastenbaum, Kubler-Ross's model is too general, and does not take account of differences between fatal conditions. For instance, some diseases are extremely painful and long, which can alter the dying process considerably. The dying person's gender, age, and socioeconomic status also have influence on the dying process. Research has shown that some people skip one or more of the five stages, and some people regress back to an earlier stage during the process of dying.

Telling a Person He/She is Dying

There is a general consensus among psychologists that a dying person should be informed completely. Although it can be difficult to tell a person that he is going to die, this knowledge gives the person a chance to settle affairs and say goodbye to loved ones. It is tragic when a person dies with much work left undone. Also, property disputes can arise when a dying person does not have a chance to settle his estate. Many terminally ill individuals derive some comfort from planning their funeral, burial, or memorial service. Finally, the acknowledgement of impending death makes it possible for a person to receive hospice services.

Brain Death

When the electrical activity of the brain ceases, brain death is said to occur. Some specialists assert that brain death may only include the cessation of the electrical activity in the higher parts of the brain, even when the lower brainstem continues to function. So long as the lower brainstem has some electrical activity, a person can still maintain respiration and circulation. However, without electrical activity in the cortex and thalamus, the person will have no real consciousness. Among most doctors, brain death is only said to have occurred when function ceases in both the higher and lower parts of the brain.

Euthanasia

Euthanasia, literally meaning good death, is the intentional ending of life, usually to prevent suffering. One common example of euthanasia occurs on the battlefield, where soldiers whose injuries are deemed to be terminal are killed by their comrades. In the modern world, there are two basic kinds of euthanasia. Active euthanasia is the intentional causing of death. For instance, in some places it is legal for a doctor to help a fatally ill patient commit suicide. In the United States, the only state that allows active euthanasia is Oregon, which in 1994 passed a Death with Dignity Act. Passive euthanasia, meanwhile, is allowing death to occur, for instance by removing a device like a respirator, or withholding potentially life-saving treatment. Passive euthanasia may be performed when a patient is in a permanent coma or has a terminal illness.

Living Will

Living wills are created so that people can make their health care wishes known even if they are incapacitated. A living will is composed while the person is still cognizant and competent. It elaborates all of the medications and procedures that the person would like to have administered in the event he falls into a coma or becomes unresponsive. Also, living wills typically have provisions for care if the person develops a terminal or extremely painful illness. The Choice in Dying organization is credited with initiating the living will practice, which in some places is called an advance directive.

Death of Spouse Statistics

The United States Census Bureau reported in 2006 that 45% of married women and 14% of married men will have endured the death of a spouse by the time they reach the age of 65. By the age of 85, 80% of women and 43% of women will have suffered such a loss. The difference in percentages can be partly attributed to the fact that women live an average of five years longer than men, and also that women are more likely to marry older men than vice versa. Also, men are more likely to remarry after the death of a spouse.

Perception, Learning, and Memory

ECOLOGICAL VIEW OF PERCEPTION

Eleanor and James Gibson developed what is known as the ecological view of perception, which in its most basic iteration states that individuals only have a sensory impression of those items in their surroundings. The objects in a person's environment have what are called affordances, which means that they afford an opportunity for interaction. The degree to which a person interacts with the object depends on his ability. For example, a child will see a hammer as something to bang against the wall, while for an adult a hammer is a tool that can be used to build an elaborate construction.

VISUAL CLIFF EXPERIMENT

In 1960, Eleanor Gibson and Richard Walk developed the Visual Walk Experiments to measure infant depth perception. In order to perform the experiment, a glass surface is placed on top of a patterned material, such that the patterned material is very close to the glass on one end and far away at the other. Perceptually, it appears from above as if the walking surface is on a sharp slope. In the test, it was found that most infants will happily crawl across the "shallow" end, but will not cross the "deep" end, even when coaxed by their mothers. In other words, infants have a natural tendency to avoid what they see as perilous heights.

VISUAL PREFERENCE METHOD

The visual preference method, advanced in part by Robert Fantz during the early 1960s, is used to measure infant visual perception. In the basic model, a child is placed in a looking chamber, above which there are two visual displays. A researcher looking through a peephole can determine which display the child is looking at. By placing different images in the displays, researchers can get a sense of the sorts of images that are appealing or innately interesting to infants. Research into the visual preference methods includes keeping records of the length of time an infant looked at each image. This experiment determined that even two-day-old infants can distinguish visual stimuli. Indeed, it was determined that very young infants would rather look at patterns than blocks of solid color.

HABITUATION AND DISHABITUATION

Developmental psychologists use the terms habituation and dishabituation to describe the response of a small child to a repeated visual or auditory stimulus. Habituation is the phenomenon in which repeated exposure to a stimulus garners less and less attention. Even seven hours after birth, many infants display habituation. If the stimulus is altered in some way, the infant will register a more pronounced response. This recovery of the habituated response is called dishabituation. In general, infants have been found to look at familiar stimuli about one-third as often as they look at new ones.

PERCEPTUAL CONSTANCY

The understanding that physical objects maintain their proportions even when visual perception of them changes is called perceptual constancy. For instance, at three months a child may have some degree of size and shape constancy. Shape constancy is the comprehension that the shape of an object is the same even though it can be viewed from different angles. Size constancy is the understanding that an object does not change in shape even though it can be viewed close-up or from afar. A full grasp of perceptual constancy does not exist until the child is 10 or 11 years old. In particular, infants seem to have a hard time applying shape constancy to objects with irregular shapes.

INTERMODAL PERCEPTION

The process of mentally combining information from at least two senses is called intermodal perception. From birth, infants display a primitive form of intermodal perception; they will turn their heads and eyes towards the origins of a sound. As the child grows older, his intermodal perception will improve. Children from 3 ½ months seem to have more interest in a person if they can both see and hear him. This indicates that a child is cognizant of a person as having both visual and auditory components.

PERCEPTUAL-MOTOR COUPLING

In developmental psychology, the relationship between perception and movement is called perceptual-motor coupling. The extent to which a child's movements are based on what he perceives can be measured through experimentation. Over the first few years of life, a child will learn to use his eyes to navigate different surfaces, reach for desired objects, and balance. At the same time, the child's movements will provide him with information about what he perceives. Handling an object teaches a child to draw correlations between vision and size, texture, and weight. Also, a child's ability to move around an object improves his understanding of size and shape constancy.

PERCEPTUAL CATEGORIZATION

Scientists have been able to demonstrate that three-month-old infants are able to group similar objects together. This ability is called perceptual categorization, a phrase coined by Jean Mandler, a psychologist at the University of California-San Diego. Perceptual categorization requires the objects to be grouped according to some physical characteristic, like color or size. This field typically emerges at about seven months of age. As the infant grows, he will develop more complex and differentiated categories. For example, a child at first may only be able to identify basic colors, but with time may be able to identify shades as well.

PERCEPTUAL SPEED IN OLDER ADULTS

The speed with which a person can react to perceived stimuli by performing a motor task is called perceptual speed. Of all the cognitive abilities, perceptual speed is the only one that steadily declines with age. This decline is caused by degeneration of the neural impulses throughout the central nervous system. By the time a person reaches late adulthood, perceptual speed can be significantly diminished. This definition is often accompanied by a decrease in working memory. Of course, not all elderly people manifest significant perceptual speed loss.

LEARNING

In psychology, learning is defined as experiences or actions that cause essentially permanent changes in behavior. Learning is not just intellectual; it is also emotional and physical. Through learning, a person adapts to changes in the environment, and achieves greater mastery over his actions. There are four basic categories of learning in psychology: instrumental conditioning or operant learning, insight learning, multiple-response learning, and classical conditioning or respondent learning. Learning takes place throughout life, beginning even in the three months before the child is born.

CLASSICAL AND OPERANT CONDITIONING

The theory of classical conditioning is in large part based on the work of Russian physiologist Ivan Pavlov. According to this theory, the relationship between stimulus and response forms behavior in the future, and can therefore be credited for learning. Pavlov's classic experiment involved ringing a bell for dogs before feeding them. The dogs associated the bell with food, and would begin to drool whenever they heard it. If the behavior causes a response that reinforces that behavior, this is called operant conditioning. Any behavior that can be changed by altering its consequences is called an operant.

Pavlov

The Russian physiologist Ivan Pavlov had his great insight when he realized that his laboratory dogs had associated the ringing of a bell with food. The dogs would begin to drool at the mere ringing of the bell, in what Pavlov called a conditioned reflex. In 1904, Pavlov was awarded the Nobel Prize for medicine. Over the next few decades, he continued his research into classical conditioning, showing, among other things, that a physical reflex can be induced by an artificial replacement stimulus.

Skinner

The American psychologist B.F. Skinner is known as one of the fathers of classical conditioning. During the 1950s and 60s, he performed extensive research on behavior reinforcement, and was able to demonstrate that positive consequences reinforce the behaviors that precede them. From this insight, Skinner created an entire theory of how human behavior could be adjusted and controlled. Skinner's work is particularly evident in modern educational theory, which centers on rewards and punishments.

Sameroff's Research into Newborn Learning

Arnold J. Sameroff conducted extensive research into infant learning. In his 1960s experiments with infant sucking, he noted a difference between suction and expression. In suction, the infant creates a vacuum and draws milk from the nipple; in expression, the child presses the nipple against the top of his mouth, squeezing milk out. Sameroff's research suggested that if only one of these techniques was viable, the infant would use that technique alone. In other words, newborns are capable of making decisions based on positive and negative reinforcement. Indeed, Sameroff was able to go on and show that two-day-old infants were capable of applying targeted levels of pressure to extract milk.

Play as Learning

In recent decades, developmental psychologists have come to the conclusion that play is one of the most important contributors to mental, physical, and social development. Also, there is a strong correlation between play and healthy family interactions. While playing, the child learns the boundaries of acceptable behavior, as well as the values and mores of the other participants. Play is a form of socialization. When adults play with children, they teach them the rules of the culture, as well as incidental lessons in language and problem solving.

Gender Identification and Learning

Gender identification is the process of learning accepted gender norms and aligning one's personality with them. Societies contribute to gender identification by assigning certain colors and types of clothing to males or females. Each society has a set of gender roles and expectations, which are transmitted explicitly and implicitly to children. Some people think that the boundaries of gender roles have weakened in recent decades, but it is certain that they still exist. By the age of three or four, most children in the United States will identify certain actions or objects as feminine or masculine.

ZPD

A zone of proximal development (ZPD) is a set of tasks that a child cannot learn by himself, but which he is capable of acquiring with help from a more advanced person. This concept was advanced by Vygotsky, who identified learning to speak and read as tasks that fall within every child's zone of proximal development at some point. One of the implications of this concept is that social interaction is necessary for development. According to Vygotsky, a child is taught by his social environment and cultural context.

Learning Theories

There are three categories of learning theory: behavioral, cognitive, and social learning. Behavioral theories rest on the assumption that behavior can be generated or managed with positive and negative reinforcement. Cognitive theories emphasize the role of information acquisition, organization, and synthesis in managing behavior. Social learning theories emphasize the importance of interaction with other people, in particular role models.

Implicit and Explicit Memory and Infantile Amnesia

Implicit memory is memory with no conscious components. For instance, people develop an implicit memory of how to read or how to tie a shoe, even though they will never think of any particular instance when they learned this skill. Explicit memory is the memory of experiences, facts, and perceptions that can be recalled specifically. Infantile amnesia is the inability to recall memories from the first two to three years of life. Infantile amnesia is believed to be a result of the immaturity of the pre-frontal lobes, which are essential for the storage of memory.

Development of Memory

Before the age of six months, children do not have any real explicit memory. However, between six months and two years of age, the hippocampus, frontal lobes, and remainder of the cerebral cortex grow rapidly. This growth is accompanied by the emergence of explicit memory. Despite this early maturation of the brain structures associated with memory, most people can't remember much before the age of eight. Following that age, an individual is more likely to remember specific events and experiences. There are different theories for the lack of explicit memory early in life: some people think the brain has not quite developed, while others credit the lack of memory on the structure of thoughts or the emotional aspect of certain experiences.

Memory in Middle Adults

Most psychologists agree that in mid-adulthood people start to experience a decline in verbal memory. However, the results of the Seattle Longitudinal Study suggest that verbal memory may be at its best when a person is in his 50s. The aging and cognition expert Denise Park believes that middle adults take longer to enter new information into memory, but are able to hang onto it longer once it is encoded. One possible cause of memory trouble is the general overload of information that occurs as a person grows older.

Short-Term Memory

The brain is capable of retaining memory for short periods and long periods. Short-term memory is very brief retention, often for an interval of only a few seconds. Repeating information helps to store it in short-term memory. Often, a person will retain a short-term memory for just a few seconds, and will never fully encode it in permanent memory. Short-term memories do not become explicit or implicit memories. As people age, they lose their capacity and efficiency in short-term memory.

Long-term Memory

Long-term memories are retained for a long interval, maybe even for the rest of the person's life. Repetition helps in the formation of long-term memories, but many of these memories are of singular events. Long-term memories may relate to the performance of certain tasks, like tying a shoe or riding a bicycle. Long-term memory tends to remain solid longer than short-term memory as people age. In particular, people seem to be good at storing long-term memories related to formative and unusual personal experiences.

Memory Strategies

There are a number of good strategies for improving memory. In rehearsal, the individual repeats the information to himself or to another person. It can be particularly useful to incorporate movements and gestures into rehearsal, as research suggests that a multisensory exposure improves recall. In the memory strategy of categorization, a person places the new pieces of information in a rhyme or in a group by type. Some people encode memories by associating them with elaborate mental images. A child's memory tends to be better when he explicitly incorporates mnemonic strategies.

Episodic Memory

Specific memories of life events are called episodic memories. The remembrance of one's own personal experience is called autobiographical memory. Interestingly, young adults have stronger episodic memory, even though they have fewer experiences to draw on. It is believed that declines in memory associated with aging are particularly significant in episodic memory. Another interesting quality of episodic memory is that people in later life tend to have clearer memories of things that happened in their teens and twenties than they do for any other time in their lives. The degree of recall also seems to be influenced by whether the memory is perceived as positive or influential in the person's life.

Semantic Memory

All of the general knowledge a person obtains through education and assimilation into a culture is known as semantic memory. Semantic memories are particular skills, vocabulary, and pieces of information. In order to be classified as semantic knowledge, information needs to be explicable. However, it is not necessary for a person to remember where they obtained a piece of semantic knowledge. Semantic memory remains largely stable as a person ages, though recall may become slower. In older adults, there are much greater rates of decline in episodic memory than semantic memory.

Working Memory, Source Memory, and Prospective Memory

Working memory is the information held by the brain in order to solve a particular problem. For instance, a person maintains a working memory of progress thus far while completing a math problem. Source memory is the recollection of where a piece of information was obtained. Source memory seems to undergo significant decline as a person ages. When the source of information is crucial or integral to the information itself, it is more likely to be recalled. Prospective memory is the memories concerning things that must be done in the future.

Metamemory

Metamemory is recalled knowledge about memory itself. In other words, meta-memories have to do with memorizing and remembering things. Once a person reaches age five or six, he knows certain things about memory, namely that some things are forgotten, that it is easy to refresh previously learned material, and that simple pieces of information are easier to memorize than complicated pieces. At the same time, a child of this age may not have mastered tricks of memory, like concentrating on the main point of a story rather than the specific language of it. In early childhood, children tend to have a poor idea of their own memories, whereas adolescents are able to assess the extent of their own memories more accurately.

Learning Disabilities

In 2004, the United States passed legislation defining learning disabilities as "disorders in one or more of the basic psychological processes involved in understanding or in using language, spoken or written, which may manifest itself in an imperfect ability to listen, think, speak, read, write, spell, or do mathematical calculations." There are a number of learning disabilities diagnosed and managed in the contemporary classroom. In particular, though, teachers focus on learning disabilities that relate to the acquisition of academic knowledge. It is important to remember that learning-disabled people are not less intelligent, and usually do not have other physical, social, or mental impairments.

Diagnosis

Learning disabilities can be hard to diagnose, but they are most likely present when a student's level of achievement in school is two or more grade levels lower than the ability he has demonstrated on a standardized IQ tests. The federal government has issued loose guidelines for the determination of learning disability, although states and local school systems are responsible for specific procedures of diagnosis and treatment. Some students are considered learning-disabled by one jurisdiction but not by others. At all times, it is important to enlist the help of doctors and child psychologists in making a diagnosis of learning disability.

Effects of Diagnosis

For some children, a diagnosis of learning disability creates a stigma, or a false impression that academic success is impossible. However, once a child is diagnosed with a learning disability, it becomes easier for him to obtain useful academic services, like tutoring and specialized instruction. Also, the diagnosis of a learning disability may improve a child's self-esteem if he perceives that once seemingly insurmountable problems can be treated and overcome. However, some children are teased or alienated from their peers after they receive the diagnosis. Also, students who have been diagnosed with learning disabilities may be held to a lower standard by teachers.

Causes

As of yet, the causes of learning disability have not been identified. Some researchers believe that learning disabilities like dyslexia are based on genetics. The precise gene that transmits these learning disabilities, however, has not been identified. Magnetic resonance imaging (MRI) and positron emission tomography (PET) scans suggest that certain regions of the brain, like the thalamus, exhibit characteristic behavior in learning-disabled people. The thalamus is responsible for directing information from the sense organs to various parts of the brain.

Dyslexia

Dyslexia is one of the more common learning disabilities. It is characterized by an inability to recognize written words. For a long time, researchers believed that dyslexia was associated with vision problems, but it is now assumed that the disorder has more to do with speech and hearing abnormalities. Specifically, brain scans indicate that dyslexics have unusual structures in the language area of the cerebral cortex's left hemisphere. Contrary to what may be assumed, individuals with dyslexia typically have average or better than average intelligence. Overwhelmingly, dyslexia afflicts males rather than females. The best treatment for dyslexia is remedial education.

ADHD

Attention deficit hyperactivity disorder (ADHD) has a number of common symptoms, like impulsiveness, inattentiveness, and excessive activity. This disorder is diagnosed in many children these days, typically in one of three varieties. If a child is easily bored and cannot stay on task, he may have ADHD with predominantly inattention. If the child acts without considering the consequences and is generally impatient, he may have ADHD with predominantly hyperactivity/impulsivity. It is also possible to have ADHD with both hyperactivity/impulsivity and inattention. Although attention deficit hyperactivity disorder may persist into adulthood, it does not rule out success in personal and professional life. However, people with this disorder are more likely to abuse substances and engage in antisocial behavior.

SUSPECTED CAUSES

The precise causes of attention deficit hyperactivity disorder are not known, though many researchers believe that it is an inherited condition. There is also the possibility that the condition is caused by problems during gestation, like exposure to alcohol or tobacco smoke. Children with ADHD seem to have below-average birth weight. Other researchers have proposed that food additives, allergies, excessive television watching, and bad parenting are to blame for the increase in attention deficit hyperactivity disorder. Brain scans indicate that children with ADHD do not develop full thickness of the cerebral cortex until three years after other children.

TREATMENT

Doctors and psychologists usually treat attention deficit hyperactivity disorder with a combination of education and behavior management. Therapy by itself does not seem to solve the problem. Perhaps one of the best solutions for children with this condition is regular and vigorous exercise. The two drugs most often used to treat ADHD are Ritalin and Adderall, stimulants that seem to focus the attention. However, there is a growing wave of criticism against administrating psychoactive drugs to children with ADHD. In particular, many critics charge that these drugs are overprescribed and often prescribed to the wrong children.

AUTISM

There are a range of pervasive developmental disorders that fall under the rubric of autism. These conditions typically manifest as repetitive behavior and trouble with communication and social interaction. Autism may be mild or severe. If it is severe, it typically appears during the first three years of life, when a child communicates poorly or performs strange behaviors repeatedly. Asperger's syndrome is a mild form of autism, in which the child communicates well but has a difficult time with nonverbal communication. Children with Asperger's syndrome are likely to develop narrow, intense interests.

CAUSES

At present, researchers do not understand the causes of autism. It is not believed that parenting can cause autism, and most authorities do not define autism as a mental illness. However, there is some correlation between autism and intellectual disabilities. In some cases, genetics seem to contribute to autism. For instance, congenital rubella syndrome, untreated PKU, fragile X syndrome, tuberous sclerosis, and fetal alcohol syndrome all correlate with autism. Vaccines containing thimerosal are blamed by some for a recent increase in autism, but this has yet to be proven by scientific testing. Brain scans have demonstrated slight abnormalities in brain structure and neurotransmitter function in the autistic brain. Also, some studies have identified a link between autism and too many or too few pieces on the DNA of chromosome 16.

TREATMENTS OR INTERVENTIONS

Autism cannot be cured, but autistic people can be taught to live healthy, fulfilling lives. As with many learning disabilities, autism is treated best if it is diagnosed early. Most autistic children require individual instruction and a high degree of order. Autistic children tend to thrive in routinized environments. It may be necessary to use behavior modification or behavioral interventions to reduce the frequency of damaging repetitive behaviors. Positive reinforcement works in some cases. Autism is not treated with medication, though related symptoms like hyperactivity or epilepsy may be managed pharmaceutically.

INTELLECTUAL DISABILITIES

Intellectual disabilities can have organic or cultural-familial causes. The organic causes of intellectual disabilities include Down syndrome, Turner syndrome, brain damage, fragile X syndrome, prenatal exposure to alcohol or drugs, environmental toxins, and malnutrition. The cultural-familial causes of intellectual disabilities are heredity and an unstimulating living environment. Some psychologists think that individuals who score between 50 and 70 on intelligence tests and who do not have brain damage may just be at the lower end of the normal distribution of IQ scores for the population.

IDEA

Responding to an education system that failed to serve disabled children adequately, the United States Congress passed the Education for All Handicapped Children Act, Public Law 94–142, in 1975. This act mandated free and appropriate public education for disabled students. In 1990, this act was updated as the Individuals with Disabilities Education Act, or IDEA. The act was amended in 1997 and reauthorized in 2004, at which point it became known as the Individuals with Disabilities Education Improvement Act. This act mandates that children be evaluated to determine whether they are eligible for special education. Also, IDEA requires schools to provide individualized education plans and the least restrictive educational environment.

IEP

Schools are required to compose an individualized education plan (IEP) for all public school students with disabilities. An IEP is a written statement describing the specific educational program appropriate for the student, based on his unique needs. The IEP should be composed by the student, his parents, an independent child advocate, teachers, and the school psychologist, in collaboration. It is considered a legal document that binds the school system to providing the outlined plan.

ATTENTION

INFANTS

From a very young age, infants are able to focus their attention on particular objects. The parietal lobes of the cerebral cortex are heavily involved in this immature attention span. In the first year of life, a child mainly focuses on objects with a view towards investigating them. Infants are capable of sustaining their attention for up to ten seconds. Infants tend to be more attentive to new stimuli. Over time, small children become habituated to repeated stimuli and pay less attention to them.

EARLY CHILDHOOD

In the preschool years, children will become much better at concentrating and prolonging their attention span. First, children will not be able to concentrate, but by the age of four or five, a child should be able to sit for a half hour and attend to a television program. This development in executive and sustained attention is not necessarily mirrored by development in salient attention and planning. This means that children can easily be distracted by more pressing stimuli, and may not be able to concentrate in great detail on the object of their attention.

JOINT ATTENTION

Joint attention exists when multiple people are attending to the same object and is required to follow a third party, to encourage other people to attend to an object, or to engage in cooperative action. One of the earliest stages of joint attention is when a child's gaze can be directed through pointing, which occurs by about seven or eight months. After about a year, an infant will be able to direct the attention of another person. The development of joint attention is crucial for learning because teaching is based on being able to persuade others to attend to certain objects.

EXECUTIVE ATTENTION, SUSTAINED ATTENTION, AND SALIENT ATTENTION

Executive attention is directed thinking related to plans and intentions, as well as to evaluating and correcting mistakes. Executive attention is necessary for monitoring and improving physical and mental tasks. Sustained attention is directed thinking that rests on a certain task, object, or event for a long period of time. Salient attention is the focus on the stimuli that are most relevant to the intended task ability to ignore loud or flashy distractions.

EFFECTS OF AGING ON ATTENTION

The process of aging exercises significant influence on attention. Research is centered on three types of attention in older adults: selective, divided, and sustained. Selective attention, the ability to limit the mind to relevant information, declines a little with age. Divided attention, used to perform more than one task at a time, also may diminish slightly, particularly when a person tries to perform more than two difficult tasks. As for sustained attention, or vigilance in attempting a certain task or objects, it seems to decline only slightly in aging adults.

INFORMATION-PROCESSING THEORY

According to the information-processing theory, development occurs as a slow expansion in mental capacity. So, instead of acquiring knowledge and skills in distinct increments, a person gradually becomes able to understand and process more complicated and sophisticated information. Child cognition expert Robert Siegler makes no distinction between information processing and thinking. He is one of the proponents of the information-processing theory, which views cognition as the perception, encoding, and representation of information. This model has had a significant effect on education, as researchers have striven to develop the best strategies for teaching students to process information.

PHASES

The three phases of information processing are encoding, storage, and retrieval. Encoding is the act of perception, identification, and memory formation. Storage is retention in the memory. Retrieval is bringing back memories accurately and comprehensively. The information-processing model is mechanistic, in that it treats pieces of information as files that are put away, organized, and later retrieved. Proponents of the information-processing model encourage students to develop sound organizational principles for information, just the way a person would clearly label files in a filing cabinet.

Cognition and Language

PIAGET'S COGNITIVE DEVELOPMENT THEORY

The cognitive psychologist Piaget outlined four specific stages of intellectual development. In the sensorimotor stage, which lasts from birth to two years of age, the child begins to understand the link between sensation and motor behavior. Between the ages of two and seven, in what is known as the preoperational stage, the child begins to incorporate symbols, most importantly those used in language. Between the ages of seven and eleven, in what is known as the stage of concrete operations, the child develops primitive reason and learns concepts about size and number. In the stage of formal operations, which begins at age eleven and goes until adulthood, the child develops abstract reasoning and a systematic approach to learning.

SUBSTAGES OF SENSORIMOTOR STAGE

In the model of development created by Piaget, the first stage, the sensorimotor stage, has six substages, beginning with birth.

- First stage, simple reflexes, the first month of life
- Second stage, first habits and primary circular reactions, from the first until the fourth month of life
- Third stage, secondary circular reactions, from four months to eight months of age
- Fourth stage, coordination of secondary circular reactions, lasts between eight and twelve months of age
- Fifth stage, tertiary circular reactions, novelty, and curiosity, between 12 and 18 months
- Sixth stage, internalization of schemes, from 18 to 24 months of age

SCHEMAS

Piaget declared that children develop a set of schemas, or structures for thinking, that enable them to interact productively with their environment. In a sense, a child's development is the process of adaptation to his environment. This process includes assimilation and accommodation. Whenever children encounter new information, they must understand that and incorporate it using what they already know: assimilation. This process stretches their schemas, however, and so there is a gradual advancement of knowledge and scope of learning: accommodation.

COGNITIVE THEORIES OF PIAGET AND VYGOTSKY

The cognitive theories of Piaget and Vygotsky share some similarities and differences. Piaget largely ignored socio-cultural context, while Vygotsky gave it a great deal of attention. Piaget could be considered a social constructivist, while Piaget is more often described as a cognitive constructivist. Vygotsky, unlike Piaget, did not outline a series of developmental stages. Instead, Vygotsky advanced such notions as the zone of proximal development, tools of culture, and the importance of language and dialogue. Piaget, meanwhile, focused on things like schemas, operations, conservation, and classification. Vygotsky placed more emphasis on language and education, but like Piaget, he believed strongly in the importance of teachers as guides rather than as lecturers.

BANDURA'S SOCIAL COGNITIVE THEORY

The American psychologist Albert Bandura, one of the leading social cognitive theorists, believed that behavior, environment, and cognition are inextricably linked. Bandura and other social cognitive theorists believe that human behavior is learned through perception and imitation. This mimetic quality to learning extends to cognition and emotion as well. In Bandura's model, there are three reciprocal elements: environment, behavior, and person/cognitive. The person/cognitive element is the most independent, and is the area in which the person exercises the most autonomy.

COGNITIVE DEVELOPMENT IN ADOLESCENTS

Adolescents undergo an intense process of intellectual development. In particular, adolescents develop the ability to construct imaginative hypotheses and possible solutions to their problems. An adolescent of normal intellectual development is able to think in the abstract and analyze data to derive a conclusion. Developmental psychologists refer to the thinking of which adolescents are capable as either formal operational thought or scientific reasoning. During this phase of life, most people develop the ability to plan for the long term and consider possible scenarios when making a decision. According to Piaget, this is the period of formal operations.

COGNITIVE DEVELOPMENT IN COLLEGE STUDENTS

For most students, the college years are a time of intense cognitive development. Of course, this development manifests in different ways for different students. In the early years of college, students have a tendency to view things as either being all bad or all good. This is referred to as dualistic thinking. As they grow more mature and gain more knowledge in class, students become capable of multiplicity in thinking, which means that they are able to consider several views of the same topic. By the time they graduate from college, students often are thinking in terms of relativism rather than positivism. In other words, students understand that truth can be different for different people and in different situations, and that any truth claims must be supported by evidence and reasoning.

PROBLEM SOLVING IN CHILDHOOD

Children learn different strategies for solving problems as they grow older. At first, children work on recognizing the different characteristics of an object. For example, it may take a child until the age of four to understand completely that objects can be grouped by color, shape, volume, etc. As a child grows older, he will become more adept at rehearsing and organizing information for use in solving problems. The development of the memory is essential for problem-solving, because the child begins to remember similar problems and how they were solved.

ADOLESCENT DECISION-MAKING

Adolescents are required to make an increasing number of decisions, and their skills for doing so increase rapidly. Beginning in adolescence, people are making decisions that will have ramifications on their entire lives, such as how hard to try in school and who to associate with socially. The adolescent brain demonstrates improvement in abstract thinking, critical analysis, and executive function. However, adolescents are still very susceptible to poor choices caused by emotions and social context and can make poor decisions related to sex, drugs, and risky behavior.

ADULT PROBLEM SOLVING

In adult life, the ability to solve problems reaches full maturity. An adult should be able to draw on their past and use their fully developed analytical skills to solve problems. Indeed, research suggests that people in their 40s and 50s are better at solving practical problems. Towards the end of late adulthood, however, people demonstrate some decline in their ability to make everyday decisions. In part, this is believed to be due to an inability to keep all of the relevant factors in a decision in mind at the same time.

THEORY OF MIND

Theory of mind is the level of awareness a child has of his own mind and the minds of others. Theory of mind is thinking about thinking; it is the recognition of one's own knowledge, desires, biases, as well as those of other people. Researchers have spent a great deal of time charting the development of theory of mind in children. At two years of age, children are not yet able to understand that another person's mind works much the same as their own. By five years of age, children can understand that other people do not have precisely the same knowledge as they do.

CRITICAL THINKING

Critical thinking is a systematic way of approaching a problem. It entails considering all of the relevant aspects of the problem, evaluating possible solutions, and ultimately coming to a decision based on evidence. Critical thinking also entails keeping the mind open to changes that might alter a decision or assumption. In order to think critically, a person needs to be able to keep various facts in mind, analyze data without prejudice, and make connections between disparate pieces of information. Critical thinking is the opposite of superficial thought. Indeed, it is a necessary condition of deep and complex understanding.

CREATIVE THINKING

Creative thinking is the unique or unusual approach to a problem. Creativity requires the mind to make uncommon associations, and to view the subject from all conceivable perspectives. Creativity is not the same thing as intelligence, because it is not aimed at coming up with the one right answer to a problem. Instead, creative thinking aims to create multiple possible solutions. A capacity for creative thought is often varies greatly in small children. For instance, some children have a great deal of creativity with language, but are not especially creative in the visual arts.

SCIENTIFIC THINKING IN TERMS OF CHILD DEVELOPMENT

Scientific thinking is slow to develop in children, though many young people show a marked interest in exploring the causes and consequences of things. Unlike scientists, who are trained to remain loyal to a theory only so far as it proves correct, children are apt to hold on to existing beliefs even in the face of contradictory evidence. In other words, children are much more attached to their inherent biases. A child is likely to pervert an experiment so that it will prove what he wishes for it to prove. As children grow, their mistaken beliefs are subjected to so much contrary evidence that they eventually must modify their thinking.

INTELLIGENCE

Intelligence is a common word, but it is a nebulous concept in psychology. In Life-Span Development, by John W. Santrock, intelligence is defined as "the ability to solve problems and to adapt and learn from experiences." Another definition offered by the psychologist David Wechsler is "a global capacity to understand the world, think rationally, and cope resourcefully with the challenges of life." According to this model, intelligence is not so much for storage of information as the ability to acquire, synthesize, and productively use information. A final definition is offered by the psychologist Robert Sternberg, who emphasized the application of knowledge in practical ways as the best manifestation of intelligence.

TRIARCHIC THEORY OF INTELLIGENCE

The psychologist Robert Sternberg developed what is known as the triarchic theory, which distinguishes analytical, creative, and practical intelligence. Analytical intelligence is the capacity for assessing information and making decisions. Creative intelligence is the capacity for coming up with unique solutions and inventing new forms. Practical intelligence is the application of knowledge in real-world situations. People may have different levels of ability in these three forms of intelligence. Many students who have high levels of creative intelligence do not do well in school because they are not as adept in analytical and practical areas.

GARDNER'S MULTIPLE INTELLIGENCES THEORY

The psychologist Howard Gardner spent his career working with gifted children, and developed a model of intelligence with nine categories. These categories are logical-mathematical, verbal-linguistic, visual-spatial, bodily-kinesthetic (related to movements and physical orientation), musical, interpersonal, interpersonal (related to self-understanding), naturalist, and existentialist (related to knowledge about fundamental aspects of life). Some critics have wondered whether all of these categories are really forms of intelligence, or whether they are simply aptitudes or skills developed by certain people.

FLUID AND CRYSTALLIZED INTELLIGENCE

Fluid intelligence: The ability to reason abstractly and handle unique and new situations. Fluid intelligence is assessed mainly with nonverbal materials, like puzzles, mazes, and block designs. Fluid intelligence tends to decline in middle adulthood.

Crystallized intelligence: Knowledge and understanding developed through education and life experience. Crystallized intelligence is typically measured with achievement testing. An individual's crystallized intelligence grows with age; it does not begin to diminish until at least the person's 60s or 70s.

GIFTEDNESS

A gifted person will score at least 130 on an intelligence test, or will demonstrate some special talent in a particular field. A gifted child will often come up with unique solutions to problems. Gifted children do not need as much guidance, because they tend to be self-motivated when it comes to their education. This is particularly true when a gifted child has a narrow area of interest, like science, music, or books. For the most part, gifted children are well adjusted socially, and do not have any mental abnormalities.

COGNITIVE STYLE

A person's cognitive style is the way he organizes and produces information. Different people find it easier to obtain information in different ways. For instance, some people prefer to have information presented visually, while others have better retention of information that they hear. Still others prefer to learn through direct, hands-on experience. In recent decades, education has begun to focus on tailoring instruction to the cognitive style of the learner. Research suggests that when people are taught in a way aligned with their cognitive style, they learn more and retain what they have learned for longer.

INTELLIGENCE TESTS

Intelligence tests like the Wechsler scales and the Stanford-Binet tests are used to predict academic performance and place children in special education classes. However, it is important not to overemphasize the results of these intelligence tests. In particular, teachers should avoid setting high or low expectations for a child based on test performance, since environmental and maturity issues can cause students to test poorly or well. Also, it should be remembered that many other factors besides IQ contribute to academic success. Extremely diligent students can often make up for poor performance on intelligence assessments. Finally, teachers should remember that all students have some strong areas and some weak areas.

IQ

Intelligence quotient, commonly abbreviated as IQ, is a measure of intellectual capacity. It is calculated by dividing mental age by chronological age and multiplying by 100. Of course, there are a number of ways to derive mental age. If a person has a mental age greater than his chronological age, his IQ will be higher than 100. If the two are equal, the person will have an IQ of 100. Intelligence quotient was first advanced as a concept by William Stern in 1912 who built on the work of the French psychologist Alfred Binet's explorations of mental age.

STANFORD-BINET TESTS

The Stanford-Binet tests are intelligence assessments. They were introduced in 1905 at the request of the French Ministry of Education. Alfred Binet and Theophile Simon were asked to come up with a way to identify children who could not learn in school. They created a test with 30 questions on a number of different topics. Since their inception, these tests have been revised in accordance with advances in the understanding of intelligence and assessment. Many of these provisions have been performed at Stanford University, which is why the tests are now known as the Stanford-Binet battery.

WECHSLER SCALES

The Wechsler scales, developed by the psychologist David Wechsler, are a set of intelligence tests for preschoolers, children, and adults. There are three separate tests: one for children between the ages of 2 1/2 and 7 years, one for children between the ages of 6 and 16, and one for adults over the age of 16. The results of the assessments are an overall score with several composite indexes indicating areas of strength and weakness. Some of these composite indexes are for information-processing speed, working memory, and verbal comprehension.

CULTURE-FAIR TESTS

In recent years, psychologists have sought to create culture-fair tests, or tests that are no more or less difficult for people from different cultures. It is important that intelligence tests assess mental capacity rather than cultural knowledge. One major criticism of standardized tests is that they are more difficult for minority students. There are two types of culture-fair test. In one type, all of the test items are composed of material that should be known to people from all socioeconomic and ethnic groups. The second type of culture-fair test, exemplified by Raven's Progressive Matrices Test, has no verbal questions at all. Psychologists have yet to develop a test that does not favor more educated people.

INFLUENCE ON INTELLIGENCE

Most developmental psychologists have beliefs somewhere in between those of the hereditarians and the environmentalists. That is, they believe that intelligence development is based on the combined influence of genetics and social/cultural context. The current consensus is that about 45% of differences in IQ are caused by heredity, 35% are caused by environment, and approximately 20% are the result of the interaction between heredity and environment. These factors are often described as genetic endowment, environmental stimulation, and covariance of heredity and environment.

GENETICS

The degree to which intelligence is determined by genetics is disputed by psychologists. So-called hereditarians believe that 60% to 80% of the differences among the general population in IQ score can be attributed to genetics. As evidence, these psychologists cite twin studies in which identical twins separated at birth score much closer to one another on IQ tests than do fraternal twins raised in the same home. Of course, there are many inherited conditions with a clear and proven influence on intelligence.

ENVIRONMENT

According to environmentalist psychologists, the context in which a person develops has more influence than heredity on his intelligence. According to these professionals, mental capacity is learned and developed based on the amount of enrichment a person receives from the immediate cultural and social environment. The psychologist Leon J. Kamin disputes the results of twin studies that seem to prove the importance of heredity, arguing instead that separated twins typically are raised in homes similar to their original home in religion and ethnicity. In other words, separated twins are not raised in especially different environments.

THEORIES OF LANGUAGE ACQUISITION
CHOMSKY'S THEORY

According to Noam Chomsky, a linguist at the Massachusetts Institute of Technology, children are born with an innate capacity for learning language. Chomsky called this a language acquisition device (LAD), and asserted that it gives the brain the ability to easily understand word and sentence construction. Brain scans have not indicated a precise location for the language acquisition device, though there is some data to suggest that parts of the brain are ideally tailored for language formation. Chomsky is considered a hereditarian or nativist thinker, because he believes that humans are born with a predisposition towards a language development.

VYGOTSKY'S THEORY

Vygotsky asserted that children do not begin by thinking in linguistic terms. At first, according to Vygotsky, children have mental functions based on their social context. A child will talk to himself while performing a task, in what is called private speech. In Vygotsky's model, private speech is an important step, because it trains the mind to structure activities and tasks in terms of language. Piaget, meanwhile, dismissed private speech as an immature form of expression, merely demonstrating the egocentrism of small children. Subsequent research has indicated that children are more likely to use private speech during the performance of hard tasks, during moments of confusion, or after making an error. Also, the use of private speech seems to correlate with better performance and more attention to instruction.

LEARNING AND INTERACTIONIST THEORIES

According to the behaviorist B.F. Skinner, language is developed in the same way as any other behavior, as the result of a long series of reinforcements and punishments. Most researchers accept this idea to some extent, though they are likely to emphasize that social interaction also plays an important role. For instance, the relationship between the child and his primary caregiver is seen to be central to the development of language. The psychologist Anthony DeCasper, whose career has centered on auditory perception in prenatal and infant children, believes that the melody of language is inculcated in a child even before birth. This accounts for the fact that children seem to be able to distinguish sounds in their own language better than they can in foreign languages.

LANGUAGE-SPECIFIC LISTENING IN THE FIRST YEAR OF A CHILD'S LIFE

Patricia Kuhl performed a series of experiments about the response of infants to sounds, and concluded that during the first six months of life a child will respond to phonemes drawn from all sorts of different languages. Between six months and a year, however, a child's ability to perceive differences in sounds from the language spoken by his parents improves a great deal. This improvement is accompanied by a diminished ability to recognize distinct sounds in foreign languages.

Sequence of Baby Language Sounds

All babies pass through a similar sequence of vocalizations during their first year. At first they cry, demonstrating three different types. The most common is rhythmic, and is believed to express hunger primarily. There are also special cries to indicate anger and pain. At about two to four months of age, a baby will begin to coo. Cooing is a gurgling sort of sound, typically uttered in pleasure. After about six months, a baby will begin to babble, or issue a series of consonants followed by vowels. The most common consonant sounds made by babies are those associated with the letters b, d, m, n, t, and w.

Receptive Vocabulary vs. Spoken Words

Even before they can speak, infants are able to understand the meanings of some words. For instance, five-month-olds often seem to recognize their own names, and by a year or so children should have a vocabulary of approximately fifty words. The words that a child understands, as distinguished from those he can speak, are called the child's receptive vocabulary. At a year and a half, a child should have a spoken vocabulary of about fifty words. Once the child reaches the age of two, he should have a spoken vocabulary of about 200 words. This rapid growth is known as a vocabulary spurt.

Language Milestones During the First 24 Months

Children of all nationalities and ethnicities go through the same milestones in language acquisition. From birth, all children cry, and after a few months all children make cooing sounds. After five months, children begin to understand particular words, and by six months most are babbling. After seven or so months of development, children demonstrate special understanding of sounds in their native language, and after about eight months a child will begin to use gestures to communicate. After a year, a child is ready to begin saying his first words. After a year and a half, the child will most likely undergo a vocabulary spurt. In the months leading up to his second birthday, the child is likely to begin uttering simple sentences.

Language Development in Preschool Children

As a child moves from age three to age six, he makes a great deal of linguistic progress. At three, children can pronounce all of the vowels and the majority of the consonant sounds, even some difficult ones like str and mpt. Preschoolers are good at noticing rhymes, and often entertain themselves by interpolating new sounds into familiar words (e.g., by saying, "ball, call, dall."). Children at this age acquire the rules of morphology and begin to use plurals and verb tenses accurately. At age four, children begin to use articles and prepositions, and incorporate alternate syntaxes to differentiate a question from a statement. During this period, the vocabulary increases markedly.

Personality Development

Freud's Psychosexual Stages

Sigmund Freud asserted that human behavior is the result of essential physical drives colliding with societal expectations. In Freud's view, the primitive drives for sex and power motivate behavior, though they are tempered by the restrictions of community. The basic personality is established by age five or six, after progression through the oral, anal, and phallic stages. Freud did not see much chance for the modification of personality over the course of life. Mainly, this is because people cannot be aware of what motivates them, much less change it.

Fixation: According to Sigmund Freud, a fixation is a state in which a person is too much enamored of the particular pleasures in one developmental stage, and therefore will not develop any further.

When this is the case, the person is likely to overindulge in certain activities. For instance, if a person becomes fixated on the oral stage, he will probably smoke too much, drink too much, eat poorly, be immature, and lack independence. A person who is fixated in the anal stage is likely to be angry and antiauthoritarian, or, if he veers back the other way, overly concerned with routines and conformity.

Erikson's psychosocial stages

According to Erik Erikson, social context is key when considering personal development. Erikson delineated nine developmental stages, and asserted that each of these stages is accompanied by a particular developmental challenge. In Erikson's terms, these are crises that give the person the potential for major growth. According to Erikson, there are points in a person's life when he must either develop parts of the personality or lose them. If these elements of the personality are lost, there will be a resulting malformation of the rest of the personality. Erikson's model was the first to address the entire span of life, rather than just childhood and adolescence.

Factors of personality

Research studies have identified five major personality factors, known as the Big Five super traits: neuroticism, emotional stability, agreeableness, extroversion, conscientiousness, and openness to experiences. In 2006, a survey of 87 longitudinal studies discovered a significant expansion of conscientiousness and agreeableness during early and middle adulthood, as well as a decline in emotional stability in this period. Early adults and adolescents seem to have more openness to experience, though this trait declines in late adulthood. People seem to undergo the most changes in the Big Five factors of personality during the early adult period.

Behavior genetics

The science of the interrelationships between behavior, heredity, and environment is known as behavior genetics. Specifically, behavior genetics is the study of how differences between people are determined by these factors. Perhaps the most famous experiments in behavior genetics are those related to twins and adopted children. Behavior geneticists often take a look at identical and fraternal twins, to see whether there are differences in behavior between individuals with identical chromosomes. Of special interest are cases in which twins were separated at birth and raised in starkly different environments. In adoption studies, meanwhile, behavior geneticists examine whether adopted children demonstrate the influence of their genes or of the environment in which they grew up. Again, the best cases for examination are often those in which one sibling is adopted and raised in a different environment.

Emotional development

First two years

When babies are born, they can exhibit the emotions of interest, disgust, and distress. The work of psychologist Carol E. Izard demonstrated that after about six to ten weeks, a child will exhibit a social smile in response to the interest and smiles of other people. After about three or four months, an infant will develop the emotions of surprise, sadness, and anger. Between five and seven months, fear seems to emerge, and a little later shyness and shame accompany the emergence of self-awareness. In the second year of life, children began to exhibit the emotions of guilt and contempt.

Middle childhood

During middle childhood, people learn to regulate their emotions in ways that are acceptable in their culture. This is in part due to increasing interaction with a broad array of people, like teachers, family members, and classmates. During these interactions, the child learns what is acceptable, and begins to understand how emotional displays are perceived depending on gender. For instance, in the United States it is generally more acceptable for boys to express anger, while it is more acceptable for girls to express sadness. It is very common during middle childhood for girls to express more empathy than boys.

Research of Ruthellen Josselson and Carol Gilligan

In the 1970s, the feminist psychologists Ruthellen Josselson and Carol Gilligan were among those who performed experiments focused on the development of the female identity. This research was in part to the work of Freud and Erikson, which was perceived as overly concerned with men. Both Josselson and Gilligan determined that female identity is created not so much in jobs or politics, but in relationships. According to Gilligan, "Women conceptualize and experience the world in a different voice, and men and women operate with different internal models." The work of Josselson, meanwhile, determined that women assign the most value to issues related to religion and social-emotional issues.

Attachment

An attachment is a strong emotional bond between people. Perhaps the most common attachment is between a mother and child. Different psychologists have come up with theories for the formation of infant attachment. For instance, Freud thought the attachment was based on food, though Harry Harlow's experiments in which baby monkeys bonded with a soft but inanimate surrogate mother without food seem to disprove this idea. According to Erikson, care and comfort provision are the most important factors in the formation of infant attachment. John Bowlby, meanwhile, advanced the theory that both baby and mother are predisposed by biology toward attachment. Moreover, Bowlby asserted that typical baby behaviors help solidify the formation of the attachment.

Phases

Developmental psychologists have performed a great deal of research on the progression of attachment. Their conclusions form a rough consensus. According to Bowlby, for instance, there are four phases in attachment: birth to two months, in which any person can elicit a smile or cry from the child; two to seven months, in which the child focuses on his primary caregiver; seven to twenty-four months, in which the child's attention expands to include all regular caregivers; and beyond twenty-four months, in which the child develops the first stirrings of empathy. Another model, derived from research with Scottish infants, has three stages: birth to two months, in which the child is responsive to the entire environment; from the third to the seventh month, in which the child responds to all people; and from seven months on, in which the child show more attachment to certain familiar people.

Adolescence

Although attachment is most often discussed in the context of infancy, people make attachments in all phases of their lives. For instance, even while adolescents are struggling for greater independence and autonomy, they also maintain strong attachments with their parents. Research has suggested that there is a moderate correlation between the attachment of adolescents and parents and the success of adolescents in peer relationships. At the same time, adolescents who have strong attachments with their parents are less likely to become juvenile delinquents or to abuse substances. It seems that adolescents who form strong attachments with their parents are better able to form romantic attachments later in life.

RAD

Reactive attachment disorder, or RAD, is diagnosed in children who have a hard time forming attachments. Such children seem withdrawn and inhibited, do not look to others for comfort, and do not seem to differentiate between caregivers. Children may also receive this diagnosis if they seek attention from all people, with no special preference for their parents or primary caregivers. There are a number of possible causes of reactive attachment disorder, including neglect during infancy, frequent changes in caregiver, and low emotional affect on the part of caregivers.

Gender schema theory

The gender schema theory asserts that children begin to create gender types as they create gender schema, or cognitive frameworks about the behaviors and characteristics that are considered masculine or feminine in their culture. In the first few years of life, a child learns to organize the world in terms of masculine and feminine concepts, according to signs received from the culture at large. Indeed, many developmental psychologists believe that differences in genitalia are less important for children than differences in perception and treatment in society. Children are consistently receiving cues related to clothing, hygiene, grooming, activities, and jobs, some of which are defined by the culture as masculine, while others are defined as feminine.

Social cognitive theory of gender

The social cognitive theory of gender asserts that awareness of gender norms is created by the observation and imitation of adults and older children. Also, children develop their awareness of gender roles through rewards and punishments. From birth, boys and girls are treated differently by most people. Moreover, boys and girls are discouraged from behaving in ways that are not considered appropriate to their gender. When children act in ways that are considered correct for their gender, they are rewarded. In these ways, children learn how they are meant to behave right from the start.

Gender cleavage

Gender cleavage, commonly referred to as gender segregation, is the tendency of children to align themselves with members of the same gender group. Gender cleavage emerges during the early school years, and continues through adolescence. Although a first grader will probably play with both boys and girls, he is likely to have a best friend from his own gender group. In third grade, gender cleavage is in full effect, though it does not peak until fifth grade. In part, gender cleavage is the result of the socialization of boys and girls in the United States. There are different roles and expectations for boys and girls, so they tend to associate with people who share those characteristics.

Development of gender roles

Through words and actions, parents communicate information about gender roles to their children. For instance, boys are often taught not to cry, with the implication that this is not masculine behavior. Also, parents participate in different activities with their children depending on gender. Boys may be pushed to participate in sports, while girls may be pushed towards participation in dance. Girls are often expected to excel in the arts, while boys are more likely to be pushed towards math and science. Parents even communicate gender information with nicknames. For instance, many of the nicknames given to boys (Rocky or Buster, for example) connote strength. Some research has suggested that there is greater enforcement of gender norms with regard to males than females.

Gender Stereotypes

To some extent, our society views certain characteristics as positive when they are exhibited by one gender, and negative when they are exhibited by the other. For instance, strength and independence are often praised in a boy, but criticized in a girl. Nurturing and empathy, on the other hand, are positive female traits that may be criticized when exhibited by a male. These stereotypes are gradually softening, as more women find jobs in politics and business, and more men take on roles as caregivers. Nevertheless, stereotypes are very persistent with regard to gender roles, and children still acquire specific expectations and role characteristics.

Gender Differences

Many of the perceived differences between genders are artificial, but there are some real differences between males and females. For instance, females tend to have more body fat than males, and tend to be smaller physically. Females tend to live longer, and have less incidence of physical and mental disorder. The brains of females and males are similar, and indeed there is no research to suggest that one or the other gender is better at math, science, or the arts. It does seem that boys are more physically aggressive, though females can be equally aggressive with their words.

Personality Changes in Late Adulthood

Even in late adulthood, the personality still undergoes subtle changes. For instance, people seem to become increasingly conscientious in late adulthood, and are often more agreeable than they were when they were young. Interestingly, some longitudinal studies have correlated conscientiousness with risk of death. However, this finding has been complicated by other studies that correlated increasing risk of mortality with high levels of neuroticism. The mortality of a person in late adulthood seems to be largely tied to his outlook on life, with optimists generally living longer than pessimists.

Peck's Psychosocial Tasks of Later Adulthood

The psychologist Robert C. Peck, in his seminal 1960s work The Road Less Traveled, advanced the theory that people in late adulthood are confronted with three challenges. To begin with, people at this age may struggle with ego differentiation versus the work-role preoccupation, which relates to how a person sees himself after ceasing employment. The second challenge, body transcendence versus body preoccupation, has to do with coping with diminished strength and health. The last challenge, ego transcendence versus ego preoccupation, is the conflict between impending death and feelings of immortality.

Erikson's Stage of Generativity

The seventh of Eric Erikson's eight lifespan stages is marked by a conflict between generativity and stagnation. This conflict typically unfolds during the 40s and 50s, as a person begins to focus on his impact on future generations. If the person perceives that he is doing nothing to aid the future, he will stagnate. Generativity may be expressed through parenting, leadership, or teaching, to name a few examples. The important thing is that an adult at this age needs to feel as if he is contributing to the long-term prosperity of his society. This seems to be accompanied by feelings of self-esteem and self-worth.

Levinson's Seasons of a Man's Life

The clinical psychologist Daniel Levinson is best known for the book Seasons of a Man's Life, which is based on extensive interviews with middle-aged men. Levinson's interview subjects were varied, from blue-collar workers to captains of industry. Through these interviews, Levinson charted the general arc of masculine life, and supported his findings with material from the biographical accounts of famous men. His conclusion was that a man passes through many stages between the ages of 17 and 65. During each of these stages, a man must master certain developmental tasks in order to progress.

ETHOLOGICAL THEORY OF DEVELOPMENT

The ethological theory of development, which emphasizes the importance of biology and evolution on behavior, was primarily advanced by the zoologist Konrad Lorenz. He studied the imprinting behavior displayed by newborn gray lag geese. He noticed that these geese follow the first moving object that comes into their field of vision. In other words, these geese were very quick to make a connection with another living creature, regardless of the identity of that creature. This observation was later expanded by John Bowlby, who proposed that children who make a strong early connection to a caregiver tend to develop better interpersonal skills. At the same time, a negative or weak connection between child and caregiver can create problems that last a lifetime.

PEER RELATIONSHIPS FOR YOUNG CHILDREN

Young children need relationships with their peers so that they can learn about emotional expression. Also, it is in these relationships that children learn how to react to the emotional displays of others. In particular, it seems to be important for children to have a safe environment in which to explore these issues. When children have supportive friendships, they tend to develop prosocial behaviors and become contributive citizens. If children have a great deal of conflict in their early peer relationships, they may become more aggressive and confrontational later in life.

PEER STATUS

Developmental psychologists have identified five peer or sociometric statuses, indicating the degree to which a child is favored by his peers. These statuses are typically determined by asking children to rate their classmates in popularity. A popular child is frequently named as a best friend, and is disliked by very few classmates. An average child receives both positive and negative reviews. A neglected child is not disliked especially, but is rarely named as a best friend. A rejected child is actively disliked and also rarely named as a best friend. A controversial child is frequently named as a best friend, but is also frequently disliked.

PEER PRESSURE

Peer pressure pushes children to act according to the norms of their peer group. Of course, the norms of the peer group may be quite distinct from the norms of society at large. For instance, adolescents are often subject to peer pressure encouraging them to smoke, shoplift, or be promiscuous. At the same time, some children are subject to peer pressure that encourages them to study hard and follow the rules. Research suggests that children feel the influence of peer pressure the most around the eighth or ninth grade. Indeed, one of the primary tasks of the years between 14 and 18 is to develop the ability to withstand peer pressure and maintain one's own system of morals.

PEER GROUPS

As a person moves from middle childhood into adolescence, his peer group becomes one of the most important factors in his socialization. A peer group can be just a few people, or it can be a large community. The peer group is typically defined by its reputation or its participation in a certain activity. For instance, a peer group could be made up of excellent students, smokers, or soccer players. A smaller group, known as a clique, contains just a few members with very similar popularity level or interests. Membership and sense of belonging to a clique is extremely important for preadolescents, but less so for older teens. By the later teen years, people seem to be less interested in group conformity, and more involved in individual and romantic relationships.

SOCIAL COGNITION IN THE RELATIONSHIPS OF CHILDREN

Social cognition is thought about relationships and interactions with other people. As children enter school and develop friendships, they must learn to handle adversarial and cooperative situations. According to Kenneth Dodge, children move through five stages in the development of social cognition. In the first stage, the child decodes social cues. Then, the decoded information must be interpreted. The child then considers possible responses. In the fourth stage, the child chooses a response. The fifth and final stage is to enact the selected response.

ANGER AND AGGRESSION

Boys and girls both feel anger, but they are taught to express it in different ways. For instance, girls exhibit physical aggression much less often than boys do, regardless of age, socioeconomic status, or ethnicity. Boys are much less adept at distinguishing an accident from an intentional wrong, and therefore are often react with aggression unnecessarily. A great deal of research has suggested that children who live in urban environments have more anger than children who live in suburban or rural environments.

AGGRESSIVE BEHAVIOR

Psychologists distinguish three kinds of aggressive behavior: undirected temper tantrums, retaliation, and verbal aggression. Undirected aggression is exhibited by children as young as one year old, though temper tantrums tend to peak around age two and decline gradually afterwards. Retaliation and verbal aggression, on the other hand, increase markedly after age three. During preschool, children seem to show a great deal of progress in regulating aggression. However, some children are less successful at this, and have a much higher probability of demonstrating violent behavior later in life.

BULLYING

Bullying is intentional and repeated aggressive behavior toward a weaker party. A bully can act independently or in a group, and may direct his behavior towards one or more people. Bullies often select their victims because of a perceived difference, like ethnicity or religion. The bullying behavior may include teasing, name-calling, sexual harassment, or even violence. Males are much more likely to engage in physical bullying, though females can be equally bullying in their verbal expressions.

CONNECTION TO VIOLENCE IN THE MEDIA

Television has been around for half a century, and research suggests that violence on the screen stimulates aggressive and violent behavior in people of all ages. Unsurprisingly, the correlation between television violence and violent behavior is strongest in those with a predisposition towards aggression. In particular, psychologists worry about the depiction of violence against women, because they believe it propagates negative stereotypes. Also, many people believe that playing violent video games and seeing violence on TV habituates people to real-life aggression.

CAUSES OF RAPE

One of the main causes of rape is the socialization of men, particularly the extents to which sex is conflated with aggression and to which women are degraded. A typical rapist is consumed by a feeling of power and general anger towards women. Date rape and acquaintance rape are becoming more common, particularly in situations where women are intoxicated. One potential cause of these problems is the male's lack of empathy with the wishes of the female. It should be noted that, although rape victims are predominantly female, there are also male victims, particularly in prison.

SEXUAL HARASSMENT

Sexual harassment is intimidating or threatening behavior that centers on sex. Sexual harassment ranges from off-color jokes and suggestive comments to physical assault. One common location for sexual harassment is the workplace, where sexual favors may be suggested as compensation for promotion or continued employment. Sexual harassment is usually perpetrated by men against women, but it can go the other way as well. Sexual harassment need not be physical or extreme; it can be the mere creation of a hostile environment for women through repeated inappropriate remarks.

MORAL DEVELOPMENT

Moral development is the process of acquiring the values, conventions, and rules of right and wrong behavior in a culture. Moral development also includes learning how to apply these abstract values to daily conduct. Morals are acquired from parents through both explicit instruction and observation. Also, children learn the morals of their society by observing community leaders, like teachers and religious figures. In large part, children learn about morals by interacting with other people, whether children their own age or adults.

THEORIES

There are a number of theories about the development of moral behavior. Freud, for instance, suggested that conscience is a natural reaction to guilt. Albert Bandura and Walter Mischel, two cognitive learning psychologists, wrote that moral behavior was learned through a process of social interactions. The developmental psychologists Piaget and Kohlberg asserted that moral development takes place at distinct stages. Piaget's model has two stages, while Kohlberg's has three levels and six stages. In the 1970s, the work of psychologist Carol Gilligan indicated that women develop morality in different ways.

Kohlberg's theory: In Kohlberg's model of moral development, there are three levels, each of which has two stages.

Level one, pre-conventional morality, is the determination of good and bad behavior that is contingent on perceived rewards and punishments.

- Stage one, obedience and punishment orientation: The child obeys the rules to avoid punishment.
- Stage two, individualism and exchange: Children behave well on the premise that it will induce good behavior towards them.

Level two, conventional morality:

- Stage three, mutual intrapersonal expectations, relationships, and interpersonal conformity: In this stage, children adopt the standards of behavior of their parents.
- Stage four, social systems morality: Behavior is based on the social order and social conceptions of justice and duty.

Level three, post-conventional morality:

- Stage five, the social contract or utility and individual rights: A person begins to focus on essential human rights.
- Stage six, universal ethical principles: A person focuses on following his conscience.

Gilligan's theory: According to Carol Gilligan and other feminist psychologists, the work of Freud, Piaget, and Kohlberg mainly applies to men. Gilligan asserted that men and women view morality differently. For example, men are more interested in justice and fairness, while women emphasize compassion and interpersonal communication. According to the research performed by Gilligan and her colleagues, women tend to interpret moral dilemmas with an emphasis on maintaining harmonious relationships. Also, female children are more likely to base their morality on the perceived behavior of other people.

PROSOCIAL BEHAVIOR

Compassionate or helpful behavior performed without expectation of compensation is called prosocial behavior. The behavior does not have to be especially active: it can be as simple as expressing interest in another person. Prosocial behavior has been observed in young children, who will spontaneously share toys and initiate taking turns on play equipment. Small children will also try to comfort another person, including a parent, who appears sad. As a person gets older, his prosocial behavior typically increases.

ALTRUISM AND EMPATHY

Altruism is positive behavior performed with no expectation of reward or personal benefit. Older children tend to demonstrate altruism more often than preschoolers. For most children, the development of altruistic behavior is accompanied by greater ability to imagine the mental lives of other people. This awareness is often called empathy. A person exhibits empathy by vicariously imagining another person's perspective, and by considering this perspective when making decisions. Compassionate and helpful behavior is often the result of empathy.

INFLUENCES ON DEVELOPMENT OF PROSOCIAL BEHAVIOR

Most psychologists believe that the primary determinant of prosocial behavior is parenting. When parents are affectionate with children, it seems to help the development of altruistic behavior, especially when children see their parents express concern for the environment and living creatures. At the same time, parents should try to avoid making their children feel guilty in order to engender prosocial behavior. Parents are important, but they are not the only influence on children. The child's culture and peer group also contribute to the formation of prosocial behavior.

STERNBERG'S TRIANGULAR THEORY OF LOVE

According to the triangular theory of love advanced by Robert J. Sternberg, there are three elements to love: passion, intimacy, and commitment. Passion is sexual and physical attraction. Intimacy is honest, close communion with another person. Commitment is the perceived desire to maintain the relationship despite potential problems. According to Sternberg, consummate love is a relationship that has high levels of all three of these components. There are other sorts of love. For instance, romantic love has passion and intimacy but not commitment. Infatuation only has passion, and fatuous love has only passion and commitment. To like someone involves merely intimacy, and empty love is commitment with neither passion nor intimacy.

Current Trends in US Marriages

Since 1970, the United States has seen a decline in marriage, both among couples with children and couples without. In 1970, over 70% of American households contained a married couple, while in 2005 just over 50% did. People who do eventually get married are remaining single for longer than ever before, and people who become divorced are remarrying at lower rates. In the first years of the new millennium, the average marriage lasted for only a little more than nine years.

Benefits of a Good Marriage

There are a number of health and happiness benefits associated with marriage. It seems that happily married people live longer and stay healthier than divorced or unhappily married people. In Japan, it was found that married women live longer. Other studies have found that married women have lower blood pressure, lower average body-mass index, lower cholesterol, and less incidence of depression or anxiety. Married men have lower risk of disease, and married men and women both report lower levels of stress. This reduction in stress seems to have beneficial effects on the function of the immune system.

Gottman's Research on Marriage

In the early 1970s, John Gottman began his research on married couples. His method entailed interviewing couples while monitoring physiological factors life blood pressure, circulation, heart rate, and immune system. Gottman followed up on these couples every year, and has to date compiled an index of over seven hundred couples. His seven studies comprise the largest database about married couples in the world. According to Gottman, love is not always an enchanted paradise. On the contrary, couples can make their marriages better and more lasting by making an effort and improving their communication.

Childbearing Trends

The average age of a first-time mother has moved from about 21 in 2001 to 25.2 in 2005. In addition, couples are having fewer children, so there is an increase in the number of families with only one child. Advances in birth control have given people more control over childbearing and family planning. At the same time, there are more institutional child-care opportunities, better parental leave offered by employers, and more male participation in child rearing and housekeeping.

Dimensions of Parenting

A series of experiments performed between 1925 and 1975 distinguished three important dimensions of child rearing. To begin with, the relative warmth or hostility of the child/parent relationship is important. Affection and approval signals warmth, while punishment and disapproval signify hostility. The second dimension of parenting is restriction when imparting morality. If parents are lax in discipline, it may lead the child toward transgressive behavior. Finally, the third dimension of parenting is consistency in the application of discipline. It is important for a parent to be consistent without being unfair.

Birth Order

In the popular consciousness, firstborn children are often expected to be intelligent, obedient, and self-sufficient. Middle-born children are expected to be friendly, outgoing, and ambitious. The last-born child is expected to be creative, willful, and less obedient. An only child is expected to be selfish and highly autonomous. Of course, these stereotypes are not always true, though researchers have noticed some alignment with them. It is believed that these personality differences may be the result of the way children are treated by the family and the society. In particular, firstborn children are likely to develop differently because they get more attention and responsibility.

ADULT SIBLINGS

Relationships between adult siblings run the gamut from intimacy to antipathy. For the most part, the relationship that siblings have as adults is similar to the relationship they had during childhood. Specifically, it is rare for children who were not close when they were growing up to become close later in life. Most sibling relationships, however, are very intimate, and remain so throughout life. While it is common for older siblings to act as authorities over younger children, this hierarchy tends to break down as siblings age.

KINSHIP CARE

Kinship care is any situation where a child is raised by someone who is close to the child but is not his parents. In most cases, the child is being raised by grandparents, although there are also situations in which an aunt, relative, or family friend raises the child. Kinship care often is required when a parent dies or is incarcerated, when a child is being abused or neglected, or when parents divorce. In the United States, the rate of kinship care has risen steadily since the 1990s.

GRANDPARENTING

The role of a grandparent is largely determined by proximity and family structure. Researchers distinguish three main styles of grandparenting. The fun-seeking style of grandparent is informal with his grandchildren, and is primarily interested in entertaining and indulging the child. The distant grandparent usually lives far away from his grandchildren, and does not have much of a relationship with them. The formal grandparent assumes the traditional role of authority figure and imparter of wisdom with respect to his grandchildren.

DUAL-INCOME COUPLES

Couples who both work must cooperate when it comes to budgeting and maintaining the home. If the couple has children, the arrangements can become even more complicated. Couples must decide who will handle the various aspects of child-rearing. In the past, it was assumed that the woman would be the primary caregiver, even if she was working full-time. Now, however, it is much more common for a man to assume an equal share of the childrearing duties. Nevertheless, most women in dual-income households report that they do the majority of the housework and child-rearing.

WORKING MARRIED WOMEN

Women who work outside the home have the opportunity to follow their interests and interact with a wide variety of people. Women who work have more financial independence and may feel a stronger sense of contributing to the livelihood of the family. Women who work often have improved self-esteem. The personal benefits of working outside the home seem largely tied to a woman's expectations; if a woman sees herself as an ambitious professional, she will not be satisfied to remain at home. Of course, the demands on the time of a working married woman are extreme.

CHILDREN'S REACTION TO DIVORCE

There are five factors that contribute to a child's reaction to divorce. Age is important, because it is related to maturity as well as custody settlements. The relative amicability of the divorce is important as well. Children whose parents remain friendly endure divorce better. Gender and custody are the third factor. In most cases, a child does better when he is in the care of the same-sex parent. The fourth factor, though, is the degree to which the custody arrangement is peaceful

and harmonious. The fifth and final factor is income, since the child's standard of living may change dramatically after a divorce.

STEPFAMILY STRUCTURE

There are three common types of stepfamily structure.

- Stepmother family: Children are cared for by their father, who subsequently remarries.
- Stepfather family: Children are cared for by their mother, who subsequently remarries.
- Blended family (also known as a complex stepfamily or reconstituted family): A marriage between two people who are already parents. Such a family has both a stepmother and a stepfather, depending on the child, as well as stepsiblings.

CHILD ABUSE AND CHILD NEGLECT

Child abuse is physical injury or harm done to a child, while child neglect is the failure to meet the child's physical, emotional, and social needs. In most cases, the perpetrators of child abuse are the child's parents or guardians. Child abuse is often physical, like shaking or hitting. It can also manifest as psychological abuse, like name-calling and excessive yelling. Child abuse can be sexual, as when a child is forced into sex or introduced to pornographic materials.

SPOUSE ABUSE

Spouse abuse, otherwise known as domestic abuse, is any behavior aimed at controlling or dominating a marital partner. Violence may be a component of abuse, but it is also possible for a spouse to psychologically and emotionally abuse his partner. A person may become isolated from his family because of spouse abuse, and may therefore lose the ability to find comfort or assistance. In most cases, the victims of spouse abuse are female. Spouse abuse can end in hospitalization or even death, so it must be treated immediately and comprehensively.

ELDER ABUSE

When an older person is treated unkindly or harmed in any way, a psychologist will diagnose elder abuse. In almost all cases, the perpetrator is a caretaker, often the victim's spouse or nurse. Older people may be abused at home, or they may be abused in an institutional setting like a nursing home or hospital. The abuse may be physical, or it may be verbal and emotional. Some of the most common and distasteful elder abuse involves exploitation, in which an elder is persuaded to change his will, to give away valuable property, or to give away power of attorney. Sexual abuse of elders is uncommon, but it does occur.

INTERGENERATIONAL RELATIONSHIPS

In almost all cultures, family is one of the most important priorities. As a person moves through life, he receives different benefits from his relationships with other members of the family. As a child, a person receives wisdom and guidance from parents, grandparents, aunts, and uncles. Later in life, the person will still be receiving guidance from parents, but will also be taking care of his children. Finally, a person sees his children move out, and must deal with aging and infirm parents. The beliefs and attitudes of a family remain remarkably consistent over time, though each generation provides its own iteration.

QUALITY CHILD CARE

The quality and formality of child care ranges widely in the United States. A good-quality child-care center will be safe and will have toys and equipment appropriate to the ages of the children. The caregivers will spend time with each child, and will ensure that the child is having his needs met. The employees of the child-care center should indicate to the children with their words and gestures that the child's desires are being considered. Children should have access to bathrooms if they are old enough, and should have their hygienic needs met by the staff if they are not.

PROBLEMS WITH NURSING HOME CARE

The nurses, therapists, physicians, and pharmacists employed by nursing homes must all meet minimum standards of competence and experience. In too many nursing homes, medication is used to sedate patients rather than to treat their illnesses. Patients may be medicated to the point that they find it hard to exercise autonomy. When this occurs, the patient's health may suffer. If patients are given appropriate care and allowed to maintain some degree of control over their lives, they tend to remain in good health for longer. It is better if patients do not become too dependent on staff.

HOSPICE PROGRAMS

Hospice programs do not try to cure patients, but instead focus on palliative care, which is the reduction of anxiety, depression, and pain. The goal of a hospice program is to allow the patient to die without relinquishing his dignity. For the most part, hospice programs are restricted to care for terminally ill and elderly patients. Hospitals often have affiliated hospice programs. Many hospice services work in the patient's home. Employees of a hospice program may be licensed to distribute pain medication and counseling about nutrition and psychology. Hospice programs often have a religious bent, though many do not. Almost all hospice programs intend to include the family of the dying individual in the decision-making process as much as possible.

COHABITING

Unmarried people who live together and have a sexual relationship are said to be cohabiting. There is a distinct trend towards cohabitation before marriage in the United States: in 1970 about 11% of couple cohabitated before marriage, and now about 60% do. Indeed, it has almost become expected in some communities for adults to live together before marriage, and many people feel that this system does a better job of predicting the future success of marriage. Many people choose to cohabitate before marriage after a bad divorce. Also, adults may choose to cohabitate rather than marry for financial reasons.

RETIREMENT

American workers spend 10 to 15 % of their lives retired. However, this percentage is decreasing as people work beyond the former retirement age of 60. Many people elect to take on another career after retirement, and many companies offer employees the option of slowly decreasing their hours after reaching their mid-60s. In part, this trend away from retirement is due to increasing cost of living. However, most people pursue a postretirement occupation that is significantly less lucrative, and indeed many people volunteer after retiring.

PROBLEMS FOR WIDOWS AND WIDOWERS

After losing his spouse, a person is likely to undergo a bout of loneliness and grief. In addition, many people suffer reduced income after the death of an employed spouse. When children are left behind, the remaining spouse has to shoulder the load of raising them, and perhaps will need to assume the role of both mother and father. When a person loses his spouse, he has a tendency to make bad health decisions, such as eating poorly or avoiding exercise. The bereaved may not sleep enough, and may abuse substances like alcohol and sedatives. Widows and widowers seem to fare better when they have a large social network.

IMPACT OF TYPE OF DEATH ON GRIEVING PROCESS

The extent to which friends and family are bereaved after the death of a loved one has a great deal to do with the manner of death. If a person dies suddenly or unexpectedly, the bereaved are likely to be in shock and then intense grief for a long time. If the person dies after a prolonged illness, the bereaved may feel relief more so than grief. People who are involved in accidents that claim the lives of others are likely to endure symptoms of post-traumatic stress disorder like nightmares, intrusive thoughts, inattention, and anxiety.

IMPORTANT TERMS

- Culture: The set of attitudes, behaviors, ideas, and beliefs that predominate among a group of people, as well as the physical acts, institutions, gestures, and manners of expression that are acceptable in that group.
- Ethnic identity: The feeling of identification and belonging with people from a particular background, including a sense of solidarity with the culture and traditions of those people.
- Socialization: The process of acquiring the cultural artifacts (values, behaviors, beliefs, etc.) of a society in order to integrate oneself.
- Independent variable: The variable in an experiment that is manipulated. In other words, the variable that is changed to see what effects that change will have on the system. Often referred to as Factor X.
- Dependent variable: The variable in an experiment that changes as a result of the manipulation of the independent variable. Often referred to as Factor Y.
- Extraneous variable: Any factors besides the independent and dependent variables that can have an effect on the results of a research study. For instance, the environmental conditions in which the experiment is performed, the health and education of the subjects, and the time of day at which this experiment is conducted.
- Cohort: A group of people with one demographic factor in common. For instance, a group of people born during a particular interval, or in a particular location.
- Random sample: A representative group of members from a population selected by some method that gave every member of the population the same chance of being selected.
- Control group: All of the members of an experiment who are not affected by the independent variable. The data generated by the control group is compared with the data generated by the group in which the independent variable is manipulated.
- Zygote: Fertilized egg cell (ovum).
- Blastocyst: Collection of cells made by cell division during the first week of a pregnancy. The embryo will be formed with an inner layer composed of the blastocyst.
- Trophoblast: Outside layer of cells on the blastocyst, which helps connect it to the wall of the uterus. The trophoblast will ultimately develop into the placenta.
- Embryo: The fetus from the time at which it attaches to the wall of the uterus until the end of the eighth week of pregnancy, when it can be recognized as human.
- Axon: Long, thin nerve fibers that extend out from a neuron, and along which information is transmitted. Many axons are covered in a myelin sheath, and may have at the ends terminal buttons, from which neurotransmitters flow into the synapses between neurons.
- Dendrite: A fiber projecting out from a cell body towards other cells. Typically has a number of branches.
- Neuron: Nerve cell that helps to communicate information around the body. The neurons in the brain process and transmit information. Nerves are ropey bundles of neurons.
- Synapse: The gap between the axon of one neuron and the dendrites of another, over which information is transmitted. Nerve cells don't come into physical contact, but are separated by synaptic gaps, across which neurotransmitter chemicals carry information.

- Myelination: The process in which a collection of fat cells encase an axon. These fat cells are called myelin, and they lubricate electrical transmissions, insulate the axon, and are believed to generate energy for the neuron.
- Sex: Male or female physical characteristics, specifically those related to reproduction.
- Gender: Social and psychological characteristics related to being a male or female. Composed of what a given culture or society believes to be masculine or feminine characteristics.
- Gender identity: A person's self-image as it relates to masculinity or femininity. In other words, the extent to which a person perceives himself as masculine or feminine.
- Gender roles: The beliefs and expectations a society or culture has for males and females.
- Phonology: System of sounds in a language, including the combination of sounds to create words. A phoneme is the smallest sound unit. There are 42 phonemes in English.
- Morphology: A language's rules for creating words. Words are made up of morphemes, which are the smallest sensible units of language.
- Syntax: The rules by which words must be ordered in a language in order to produce sensible sentences and phrases.
- Semantics: The meanings or definitions of words.
- Pragmatics: The alteration or adjustment of language for particular situations or contexts.
- Reflexive smile: Unprompted by stimuli. For instance, the smile that passes over the face of a sleeping infant.
- Social smile: Prompted by external stimuli, as for instance a familiar face or voice. Two-month-olds may demonstrate social smiling.
- Stranger anxiety: Fear of unfamiliar people. Typically does not manifest until between six months and a year.
- Separation protest: The cries of an infant forced to part ways with a caregiver.
- Grief: A state of sadness following the death of a friend or family member. A grieving individual is often numb and empty, and may vacillate between sadness and rage. During grief, a person is likely to experience intense yearning for the deceased.
- Prolonged grief: An extremely long bout of grief, characterized by numbness or detachment, and endured by between 10 and 20% of those who lose a loved one. In prolonged grief, the person often feels negative about life in general, and may become physically and mentally depressed.
- Bereavement: The time immediately following the death of a loved one. The people left behind are called the bereaved, and are likely to be grieving. Different cultures have different expectations for the behavior and conduct of the bereaved.
- Mourning: The cultural practices related to behavior after the death of a loved one. Some common gestures of mourning are wailing, wearing black, holding a funeral, and chanting. Many cultures have very specific requirements for mourning. For instance, some cultures insist on cremation, while burial is the norm in others.
- Microsystem: The network of social ties in a person's life, as for instance family, friends, and colleagues. Also, the physical environment in which those ties exist.
- Mesosystem: The manner in which a person's microsystems interact. For instance, the relationship between a person's work environment and their family life.
- Exosystem: All of the social mechanisms that affect a person's behavior. For example, relationships based on religious affiliation can affect behavior at work.
- Macrosystem: The general culture in which a person lives, including the prevailing economic, political, religious, and social mores.

DSST Practice Test

1. A correlative method of studying child behavior indicates what type of question?
   a. which comes first?
   b. what goes with what?
   c. who did what?
   d. why did that happen?

2. Time sampling is a type of...
   a. systematic observation.
   b. semi-clinical interview.
   c. sondage.
   d. spontaneous conviction.

3. According to Piaget, when a child's answer to a question is the result of careful thought, it can be termed...
   a. romancing.
   b. suggested conviction.
   c. answers at random.
   d. liberated conviction.

4. Children who are very susceptible to external stimuli, may be called what?
   a. field dependent
   b. field independent
   c. externally dependent
   d. internally impaired

5. What was the focus of Jean Piaget's theory of development?
   a. physiological development
   b. speech development
   c. cognitive development
   d. psychosocial development

6. Which of the following theorists focused primarily on psychosocial development?
   a. B.F. Skinner
   b. Sigmund Freud
   c. Erik Erikson
   d. Jean Piaget

7. What does the "cultural drift hypothesis" address?
   a. effect rather than cause
   b. cause rather than effect
   c. neither cause nor effect
   d. both cause and effect

8. If a research project involves naturalistic observation, does the researcher need to obtain informed consent from the subjects involved?
    a. no, consent is never needed with naturalistic observation
    b. yes, informed consent must always be obtained
    c. yes, but only if it can be obtained without the subject's knowledge of the type of research being done.
    d. no, if the research can be reasonably assumed to not be harmful

9. When does the blastocyst period take place?
    a. from fertilization until the fifteenth week of development
    b. from the third week until the eighth week of development
    c. from the tenth week until the twelfth week of development
    d. from fertilization until approximately the fifteenth day of development

10. A fontanelle is...
    a. an early development in the first stage of pregnancy.
    b. an irregular indentation at the base of an infant's skull.
    c. the soft spot on the top of an infant's head.
    d. a treatment used for PKU after birth.

11. What is lallation?
    a. repetitive sounds a child makes
    b. the process of a mother producing human milk
    c. a treatment modality for new mothers
    d. the initial stage of speech development

12. Which of the following are female sex hormones?
    a. progesterone and estrogen
    b. testosterone and progesterone
    c. androgens and estrogen
    d. estrogen and testosterone

13. According to Masters & Johnson, how many stages of sexual response are there?
    a. two
    b. three
    c. four
    d. five

14. What function of the nervous system keeps the body in balance?
    a. peripheral adjustments
    b. somatic responses
    c. homeostasis
    d. cerebellum

15. The pinna, meatus and malleus are parts of which sensory organ?
    a. the skin
    b. the mouth
    c. the eyes
    d. the ear

16. **The cephalocaudal principle refers to the idea that...**
    a. development progresses from head to toe.
    b. development progresses from toe to head.
    c. development is a complex process.
    d. development is a time-intensive process.

17. **According to Elisabeth Kubler-Ross' stages of death and dying, most people go through how many stages in dealing with imminent death?**
    a. two
    b. three
    c. four
    d. five

18. **Disengagement theory says that an elderly individual will be happiest if he...**
    a. keeps as active as possible.
    b. gradually withdraws from life.
    c. forms many personal relationships.
    d. learns new things.

19. **Eric Lenneberg, a proponent of the "critical-period" theory of language development, believed that language development correlated less with age and more with...**
    a. critical-sensation acquisition.
    b. visual acuity.
    c. motor development.
    d. I.Q.

20. **Which of the following would be associated with learning theory?**
    a. Watson
    b. Freud
    c. Rogers
    d. Alberts

21. **Memory operates using three basic steps. Which of the following is the first step?**
    a. encoding
    b. storage
    c. transfer
    d. retrieval

22. **Which of the following is a type of sensory memory specifically involving vision?**
    a. echoic memory
    b. long-term memory
    c. iconic memory
    d. short-term memory

23. **Dyslexia is a...**
    a. developmental reading disorder.
    b. developmental writing disorder.
    c. developmental attention disorder.
    d. developmental arithmetic disorder.

24. If a child demonstrates impulsivity, inattention and hyperactivity, he may be diagnosed with which of the following?
    a. ADHD
    b. dyslexia
    c. dysgraphia
    d. dyscalculia

25. In information processing, an individual uses a rule of thumb to reach a conclusion. To what does this type of problem solving refer?
    a. evaluation
    b. an algorithm
    c. a heuristic
    d. production

26. A child watches her mother drying dishes. She picks up a towel and cup, and begins to dry the dish as well. Which type of behavior might this indicate?
    a. cognitive map
    b. biofeedback
    c. self-reinforcement
    d. modeling

27. A toddler is praised by her mother each time she puts her toys back in her toy chest, so she continues to put her toys away each night. Which type of learning is this?
    a. operant conditioning
    b. classical conditioning
    c. cognitive learning
    d. Pavlovian

28. Stimulus generalization is...
    a. a Pavlovian concept.
    b. a Freudian concept.
    c. a Bandura construct.
    d. a Rogerian therapy technique.

29. Extinction refers to eliminating a behavior through...
    a. positive stimuli.
    b. aversive stimuli.
    c. removing a reinforcement.
    d. reinforcement.

30. Even though he has never been trained in CPR, a young man saves the life of someone who has collapsed by using the basic CPR techniques. This is most likely an example of...
    a. a very high I.Q.
    b. heroic tendencies.
    c. latent learning.
    d. symbiotic association.

31. Janie has watched her mother knit for years. One day she decides to try knitting, and is surprised to discover that she is able to knit. Which type of learning might this be called?
   a. observational learning
   b. latent learning
   c. symbiotic association
   d. biofeedback learning

32. In what might an electromyography, electroencephalograph and blood pressure cuff be used?
   a. Rogerian intervention
   b. intensive psychotherapy
   c. hypnotherapy
   d. biofeedback

33. When an individual believes that nothing they do can affect what happens to them or their environment, it is called...
   a. observational learning.
   b. learned helplessness.
   c. learned ineffectiveness.
   d. inability to thrive.

34. In terms of memory, "clustering" refers to...
   a. placing information into higher order categories.
   b. placing information into lower order categories.
   c. organizing information according to alphabet only.
   d. organizing information according to color only.

35. Children achieve "conservation" during which Piaget stage?
   a. formal operational
   b. sensorimotor
   c. concrete operations
   d. preoperational

36. A child's first spoken words conveying a complete thought are called...
   a. motherese.
   b. telegraphic speech.
   c. alliteration.
   d. holophrases

37. What is a "language acquisition device"?
   a. our inborn ability to acquire language
   b. a standard treatment for dyslexia
   c. a machine used to aid children with developmental problems
   d. a technique to minimize stuttering

38. Which is a type of language commonly used between mother and child?
   a. MLU
   b. LAD
   c. motherese
   d. alliteration

39. A barrier to problem solving discussed by Karl Duncker is called what?
   a. heuristic
   b. algorithm
   c. functional fixedness
   d. evaluation

40. According to Teresa Amabile's analysis of research on creativity, which of the following can make a person more creative?
   a. intrinsic motivation
   b. a high-paying job
   c. parenthood
   d. a stress-free life

41. What is aphasia?
   a. a visual deficit
   b. an auditory disability
   c. a language disturbance
   d. a mobility issue

42. To what does "androgynous" refer?
   a. a balance of both masculine and feminine characteristics
   b. a predominantly feminine individual
   c. a predominantly masculine individual
   d. a male with more feminine qualities than is the norm

43. The theory that how we think is affected by our choice of the language we use is called...
   a. a language acquisition device.
   b. the linguistic-relativity hypothesis.
   c. nativism.
   d. language resemblance.

44. When thoughts and actions are incompatible, it is called...
   a. a semantic differential.
   b. cognitive consistency.
   c. an inferiority complex.
   d. cognitive dissonance.

45. Piaget's concept of "imminent justice" referred to...
   a. the court system's response to adolescent criminal behavior.
   b. adult female moral aptitude.
   c. the moral attitude of adult males.
   d. the moral development of children.

46. Which of the following states are believed to be the healthiest?
    a. single
    b. legally separated
    c. married
    d. widowed

47. A ten-year-old, upon the birth of a baby brother, begins sleeping with his baby blankie again. What might this behavior be called?
    a. regression
    b. repression
    c. projection
    d. sublimation

48. Sigmund Freud theorized that the id...
    a. was our common sense.
    b. operates on the "perfection principle."
    c. was our moral taskmaster.
    d. represented our basic needs.

49. Freud said that gender identity is a result of...
    a. identification with the same sex parent.
    b. identification with the same sex peer group.
    c. the id.
    d. instinct.

50. What do social learning theorists say causes aggression?
    a. rewards and punishments only
    b. rewards, punishments and society
    c. society only
    d. internalized factors only

Answer Key and Explanations

1. B: Correlative methods try to determine which variables go together. Such a method seeks to make connections, such as "at what age do children first make eye contact regularly?" or "how many words do children speak at a given age?" The correlation coefficient can range from -1.00 to +1.00, and the outcome of a correlational study is either positive, negative or has no correlation.

2. A: Time sampling is a type of systematic observation that involves the researcher noting the number of times a particular behavior occurs within a given time frame. There are different types of time sampling, including momentary time sampling (MTS) and partial interval (PI) sampling.

3. D: Piaget describes answers that are from the depths of the child's mind as liberated conviction. These are very useful types of responses. On the other hand, romancing (making up an answer without thinking), suggested conviction (answers to please the researcher) and answers at random, are three types of reply that are of little value.

4. A: Field dependent and field independent are cognitive styles. A field independent child might be said to be able to deal with distracting, external stimuli more effectively than the field dependent child, who is significantly affected by external distractions.

5. C: Jean Piaget focused on cognitive development, and formulated a series of four stages to explain a child's level of ability at certain age ranges. The stages are sensorimotor, preoperational, concrete operations and formal operations. He also focused on the role of maturation and experience in a child's development.

6. C: Erikson was a psychoanalyst who developed the only major theory that covered normal human development and also took into account the entire human lifespan. He formulated eight stages of development, each of which is dependant upon the resolution of a crisis. His stages are "basic trust vs. basic mistrust", "autonomy vs. shame and doubt", "initiative vs. guilt", "industry vs. inferiority", "identity vs. role confusion", "intimacy vs. isolation", "generativity vs. stagnation" and "basic integrity vs. basic despair."

7. A: The cultural drift hypothesis considers the possibility that one particular variable may be the effect of another variable, rather than the assumed cause. For example, individuals with lower than average intellectual abilities may often be seen in a lower socioeconomic class. One might assume that the intellectual level is caused by the economic conditions in which the person lives. However, cultural drift hypothesis would suggest that those with low intellectual ability may "drift" toward the lower socioeconomic status, making the economic situation an effect of the lower intellect.

8. D: Put simply, you can dispense with informed consent if the research won't cause harm, or where permitted by law or the regulations of the institution. Within these simple guidelines are more specific specifications, but those are the general considerations.

9. D: The zygote produces cells and moves down the fallopian tubes until it eventually attaches itself to the uterine wall. The zygote then produces structures, such as the chorion, to provide nourishment and growth.

10. C: An infant's bones are softer and shaped differently at birth than those of an adult. The fontanelle is a soft spot on the top of an infant's head where the bones of the skull are not yet fully fused together. The bones will fuse together between nine months and a year of age, forming a completely hard skullcap.

11. A: At around six to eight months of age, the child enters into a late stage of babbling, and progresses from there to making repetitive sounds, such as ba-ba, la-la, and ma-ma. This repetitive vocalization is termed lallation, which includes both vowel and consonant sounds. This type of behavior shows the child's progress at making sounds that are a more focused attempt at direct communication.

12. A: The two major female sex hormones are progesterone and estrogen. Both have been linked specifically to sexual arousal in animals, and the human female may be more likely to be interested in sexual intercourse when levels of the hormones are at their highest. Androgens and testosterone are both male sex hormones.

13. C: Masters & Johnson were a pioneering team in researching human sexuality. They identified four stages of sexual response based on vasocongestion (blood flow), and myotonia (muscle contraction). The four stages are excitement, plateau, orgasm and resolution. A number of identified behaviors have been detailed for each of these stages, and difficulties can arise at any time during the four stages because of a number of factors.

14. C: Homeostasis refers to an assortment of automatic adjustments to important bodily functions by the autonomic nervous system. It ensures the "balance" that is necessary for survival. For example, when the body gets too hot, it begins to sweat. If the temperature turns cold, the body begins to shiver. Adjustments are made all the time to keep the body in equilibrium.

15. D: The pinna refers to the outer ear, the meatus (or "auditory meatus") is the ear canal, and the malleus is the "hammer" (the bone that is nudged when the eardrum vibrates). Each of these is a part of the auditory/hearing sense.

16. A: The cephalocaudal principle refers to the idea that development progresses from head to toe. In other words, development begins with the upper parts of the body, and later moves to the lower parts of the body.

17. D: Elizabeth Kubler-Ross, a pioneer in the study of death and dying, said there are five stages an individual commonly goes through in coming to terms with imminent death. Those stages are denial, anger, bargaining, depression, and acceptance.

18. B: Disengagement theory says that people will be happier at the end of their lives if they gradually disengage from it. In other words, this theory would recommend that an elderly individual involve himself in fewer activities, spend more time alone, and minimize personal relationships.

19. C: Lenneberg felt that motor development was a good indicator of maturity level, and thus correlated better with language development than the chronological age of the individual.

20. A: John B. Watson is often called the "father of behaviorism" and is associated with learning theory. He was the first to study the effect of learning on behavior. He felt that only those behaviors that are observable, rather than thoughts and feelings, are significant.

21. A: Encoding is the first step in how memory works, and is the process of putting information into some meaningful order. There are a number of ways to do this, such as encoding by sound or meaning, or making associations between new material and previously remembered information.

The second step to memory is storage (to make sure the material stays in memory), and retrieval (the ability to get the material out of storage).

22. C: The type of sensory memory that specifically involves vision is called iconic memory. Iconic memory, just as it sounds, is memory of what you see. It is not as enduring as echoic memory, which is a memory of information obtained through the sense of hearing.

23. A: Dyslexia is a developmental reading disorder most often characterized by reading difficulties as well as trouble differentiating particular sounds in verbal language. A common symptom is the reversal of letters and numbers when writing. General disorganization and memory issues are among some of the other symptoms one might see with a dyslexia diagnosis.

24. A: Attention Deficit Hyperactivity Disorder (ADHD) is one of the more common of the childhood disorders. A child with ADHD may have difficulty focusing and maintaining attention, become easily confused, be late with school assignments, be impatient and constantly in motion, as well as exhibiting other possible symptoms.

25. C: Unlike an algorithm, which is a strategy by which the individual tries every possible way to find the answer to a problem, the heuristic is far more limited. With a heuristic approach, a general rule of thumb is used to reach the solution. A heuristic approach may find an answer more quickly than the algorithm, but while quicker (when it's effective), it may not find the answer at all.

26. D: Modeling is a type of observational learning, and according to Bandura, consists of four basic steps. Those steps include perceiving the significant details of the behavior, remembering the behavior, converting the perceived information into action, and being motivated to engage in the behavior. Modeling can be a big influence on behavior and is also used in therapeutic approaches.

27. A: Operant conditioning is a type of associative learning that involves the consequences of the behavior. If the consequences of the behavior are positive, then the behavior is likely to be repeated. If the consequences of the behavior are negative, then the likelihood is that the behavior will not be repeated.

28. A: Sometimes a conditioned response is transferred to a stimulus that is similar to, but not the same as, the stimulus originally paired with the unconditioned one. This is an associative learning concept that came out of Pavlov's work with classical conditioning.

29. C: Extinction means eliminating a previous behavior. It is accomplished by no longer reinforcing a response, but can also be accomplished via punishment. An intermittently reinforced behavior will take longer to extinguish than a continually reinforced behavior. Likewise, a fixed reinforcement schedule is easier than a variable one.

30. C: Latent learning describes a type of learning that is not evident until the individual is properly motivated to exhibit it. In our example, the young man may not have even realized he knew how to do CPR, but just from seeing others do it or hearing about it, he was able to react appropriately in an emergency situation.

31. A: As in our example, people can learn by simply watching others do something. Imitating what one observes another person doing has been shown to be effective in the development of many types of behavior, including children learning simple social behaviors and aggressive behavior.

32. D: In biofeedback, people learn to recognize and control their own physiological processes. It develops an enhanced awareness of what one's body is doing and how outside influences affect the body. The aids/machines used in biofeedback can be used to inform the individual of changes in brain activity, muscle contractions and blood pressure among other factors.

33. B: Learned helplessness is the belief that the self or one's environment cannot be affected by what the individual does. The term is used in relation to both animals and humans. An outcome of this belief system is that the individual, without the motivation to try, does not learn any responses that can affect change.

34. A: An example would be someone who had to remember a list of several animals, and as an aid to memory, clusters all the dogs into one group and all the cats into another. Individuals who cluster information are more likely to remember it accurately at a later time.

35. C: Conservation refers to the ability to know that something remains the same even though its appearance may change. Piaget believed that this is not achieved in children until the concrete operational stage, which takes place from age seven to eleven.

36. D: A sound made by the child that can have several meanings, but is interpreted at the time it is uttered to convey a particular message, is called a holophrase. Holophrases are the first spoken words and can communicate a complete thought in just one word.

37. A: A language acquisition device was theorized by Noam Chomsky. He said that the human brain is constructed in such a way that it gives humans the ability to talk in much the same way as they are naturally able to learn to walk.

38. C: Motherese is a type of language often used between mother and child. Using fewer pronouns and verbs, repeating key ideas and raising the pitch of the voice, are a few characteristics of "motherese". In order to develop fluent language skills, children need to have adults speak to them, and therefore motherese can be an important part of language development.

39. C: Functional fixedness happens when an individual relies too heavily on previously used ways of dealing with problems. This overreliance inhibits the ability to reach novel solutions, and therefore makes problem solving more difficult.

40. A: Amabile's review found six factors that can enhance creativity in an individual. Those six factors are intrinsic motivation (doing something because one wants to), choice, stimulation, inspirational models, freedom from evaluation (no fear of being judged), and independence (no fear of being observed and criticized).

41. C: Aphasias often occur as a result of damage to the brain in the left hemisphere, where language abilities are affected. This can be due to a stroke, head injury or other injury-inducing incidents. The type of aphasia depends upon where exactly in the left hemisphere the damage occurs and the extent of that damage.

42. A: Sandra Bern theorized that the healthiest individual is one who has a balance of the positive, gender stereotyped characteristics of both male and female. When both types of characteristics are well integrated, she calls this person "androgynous."

43. B: The linguistic-relativity hypothesis, sometimes also called the Whorfian hypothesis, theorizes that words do not simply communicate thoughts, but also that they shape those thoughts. Likewise, the use of a different language can alter how one perceives the world.

44. D: Cognitive dissonance occurs when an individual's thoughts and actions are incompatible, or when incompatible opinions are held. This state causes psychological discomfort, which can be eased through change that brings about harmony.

45. D: Piaget explored the concept of imminent justice in relation to the moral development of children. More specifically, imminent justice refers to the tendency of children to believe that if someone is hurt while doing something bad, that negative result is actually "punishment" for the bad behavior.

46. C: Research seems to indicate that people who are married tend to be physically healthier. It may also be that healthier individuals are more likely to marry and stay married. Whichever is the case, it seems that there is a positive correlation between marriage and health.

47. A: Regression is a Freudian defense mechanism, one of several ways in which the individual deals unconsciously with anxiety. In our example, the ten-year-old is likely feeling anxiety over the new addition to the family, and therefore regresses to a previous state where he felt more secure in his position in the family.

48. D: Freud theorized that the personality was composed of three parts, the id, ego and superego. The id represented the basic needs of the individual, such as the need for food and sex. The id operates on the "pleasure principle" and, just as it sounds, refers to the id's demand for immediate gratification of those basic needs.

49. A: Sigmund Freud said that gender identity is the result of identification with the same sex parent, and also due to the child's anatomy. This view is a part of his psychoanalytic theory, and was the first significant attempt to address the issue of gender identity in development.

50. B: Social learning theorists say that people learn to be aggressive for two basic reasons. They learn aggression through a series of rewards and punishments from interaction with others, both inside and outside the home. Societal attitudes also play a part in the acquisition of aggressive behavior through societal views of acceptable levels of aggression.

How to Overcome Test Anxiety

Just the thought of taking a test is enough to make most people a little nervous. A test is an important event that can have a long-term impact on your future, so it's important to take it seriously and it's natural to feel anxious about performing well. But just because anxiety is normal, that doesn't mean that it's helpful in test taking, or that you should simply accept it as part of your life. Anxiety can have a variety of effects. These effects can be mild, like making you feel slightly nervous, or severe, like blocking your ability to focus or remember even a simple detail.

If you experience test anxiety—whether severe or mild—it's important to know how to beat it. To discover this, first you need to understand what causes test anxiety.

Causes of Test Anxiety

While we often think of anxiety as an uncontrollable emotional state, it can actually be caused by simple, practical things. One of the most common causes of test anxiety is that a person does not feel adequately prepared for their test. This feeling can be the result of many different issues such as poor study habits or lack of organization, but the most common culprit is time management. Starting to study too late, failing to organize your study time to cover all of the material, or being distracted while you study will mean that you're not well prepared for the test. This may lead to cramming the night before, which will cause you to be physically and mentally exhausted for the test. Poor time management also contributes to feelings of stress, fear, and hopelessness as you realize you are not well prepared but don't know what to do about it.

Other times, test anxiety is not related to your preparation for the test but comes from unresolved fear. This may be a past failure on a test, or poor performance on tests in general. It may come from comparing yourself to others who seem to be performing better or from the stress of living up to expectations. Anxiety may be driven by fears of the future—how failure on this test would affect your educational and career goals. These fears are often completely irrational, but they can still negatively impact your test performance.

Elements of Test Anxiety

As mentioned earlier, test anxiety is considered to be an emotional state, but it has physical and mental components as well. Sometimes you may not even realize that you are suffering from test anxiety until you notice the physical symptoms. These can include trembling hands, rapid heartbeat, sweating, nausea, and tense muscles. Extreme anxiety may lead to fainting or vomiting. Obviously, any of these symptoms can have a negative impact on testing. It is important to recognize them as soon as they begin to occur so that you can address the problem before it damages your performance.

The mental components of test anxiety include trouble focusing and inability to remember learned information. During a test, your mind is on high alert, which can help you recall information and stay focused for an extended period of time. However, anxiety interferes with your mind's natural processes, causing you to blank out, even on the questions you know well. The strain of testing during anxiety makes it difficult to stay focused, especially on a test that may take several hours. Extreme anxiety can take a huge mental toll, making it difficult not only to recall test information but even to understand the test questions or pull your thoughts together.

Effects of Test Anxiety

Test anxiety is like a disease—if left untreated, it will get progressively worse. Anxiety leads to poor performance, and this reinforces the feelings of fear and failure, which in turn lead to poor performances on subsequent tests. It can grow from a mild nervousness to a crippling condition. If allowed to progress, test anxiety can have a big impact on your schooling, and consequently on your future.

Test anxiety can spread to other parts of your life. Anxiety on tests can become anxiety in any stressful situation, and blanking on a test can turn into panicking in a job situation. But fortunately, you don't have to let anxiety rule your testing and determine your grades. There are a number of relatively simple steps you can take to move past anxiety and function normally on a test and in the rest of life.

Physical Steps for Beating Test Anxiety

While test anxiety is a serious problem, the good news is that it can be overcome. It doesn't have to control your ability to think and remember information. While it may take time, you can begin taking steps today to beat anxiety.

Just as your first hint that you may be struggling with anxiety comes from the physical symptoms, the first step to treating it is also physical. Rest is crucial for having a clear, strong mind. If you are tired, it is much easier to give in to anxiety. But if you establish good sleep habits, your body and mind will be ready to perform optimally, without the strain of exhaustion. Additionally, sleeping well helps you to retain information better, so you're more likely to recall the answers when you see the test questions.

Getting good sleep means more than going to bed on time. It's important to allow your brain time to relax. Take study breaks from time to time so it doesn't get overworked, and don't study right before bed. Take time to rest your mind before trying to rest your body, or you may find it difficult to fall asleep.

Along with sleep, other aspects of physical health are important in preparing for a test. Good nutrition is vital for good brain function. Sugary foods and drinks may give a burst of energy but this burst is followed by a crash, both physically and emotionally. Instead, fuel your body with protein and vitamin-rich foods.

Also, drink plenty of water. Dehydration can lead to headaches and exhaustion, especially if your brain is already under stress from the rigors of the test. Particularly if your test is a long one, drink water during the breaks. And if possible, take an energy-boosting snack to eat between sections.

Along with sleep and diet, a third important part of physical health is exercise. Maintaining a steady workout schedule is helpful, but even taking 5-minute study breaks to walk can help get your blood pumping faster and clear your head. Exercise also releases endorphins, which contribute to a positive feeling and can help combat test anxiety.

When you nurture your physical health, you are also contributing to your mental health. If your body is healthy, your mind is much more likely to be healthy as well. So take time to rest, nourish your body with healthy food and water, and get moving as much as possible. Taking these physical steps will make you stronger and more able to take the mental steps necessary to overcome test anxiety.

Mental Steps for Beating Test Anxiety

Working on the mental side of test anxiety can be more challenging, but as with the physical side, there are clear steps you can take to overcome it. As mentioned earlier, test anxiety often stems from lack of preparation, so the obvious solution is to prepare for the test. Effective studying may be the most important weapon you have for beating test anxiety, but you can and should employ several other mental tools to combat fear.

First, boost your confidence by reminding yourself of past success—tests or projects that you aced. If you're putting as much effort into preparing for this test as you did for those, there's no reason you should expect to fail here. Work hard to prepare; then trust your preparation.

Second, surround yourself with encouraging people. It can be helpful to find a study group, but be sure that the people you're around will encourage a positive attitude. If you spend time with others who are anxious or cynical, this will only contribute to your own anxiety. Look for others who are motivated to study hard from a desire to succeed, not from a fear of failure.

Third, reward yourself. A test is physically and mentally tiring, even without anxiety, and it can be helpful to have something to look forward to. Plan an activity following the test, regardless of the outcome, such as going to a movie or getting ice cream.

When you are taking the test, if you find yourself beginning to feel anxious, remind yourself that you know the material. Visualize successfully completing the test. Then take a few deep, relaxing breaths and return to it. Work through the questions carefully but with confidence, knowing that you are capable of succeeding.

Developing a healthy mental approach to test taking will also aid in other areas of life. Test anxiety affects more than just the actual test—it can be damaging to your mental health and even contribute to depression. It's important to beat test anxiety before it becomes a problem for more than testing.

Study Strategy

Being prepared for the test is necessary to combat anxiety, but what does being prepared look like? You may study for hours on end and still not feel prepared. What you need is a strategy for test prep. The next few pages outline our recommended steps to help you plan out and conquer the challenge of preparation.

STEP 1: SCOPE OUT THE TEST

Learn everything you can about the format (multiple choice, essay, etc.) and what will be on the test. Gather any study materials, course outlines, or sample exams that may be available. Not only will this help you to prepare, but knowing what to expect can help to alleviate test anxiety.

STEP 2: MAP OUT THE MATERIAL

Look through the textbook or study guide and make note of how many chapters or sections it has. Then divide these over the time you have. For example, if a book has 15 chapters and you have five days to study, you need to cover three chapters each day. Even better, if you have the time, leave an extra day at the end for overall review after you have gone through the material in depth.

If time is limited, you may need to prioritize the material. Look through it and make note of which sections you think you already have a good grasp on, and which need review. While you are studying, skim quickly through the familiar sections and take more time on the challenging parts.

Write out your plan so you don't get lost as you go. Having a written plan also helps you feel more in control of the study, so anxiety is less likely to arise from feeling overwhelmed at the amount to cover.

STEP 3: GATHER YOUR TOOLS

Decide what study method works best for you. Do you prefer to highlight in the book as you study and then go back over the highlighted portions? Or do you type out notes of the important information? Or is it helpful to make flashcards that you can carry with you? Assemble the pens, index cards, highlighters, post-it notes, and any other materials you may need so you won't be distracted by getting up to find things while you study.

If you're having a hard time retaining the information or organizing your notes, experiment with different methods. For example, try color-coding by subject with colored pens, highlighters, or post-it notes. If you learn better by hearing, try recording yourself reading your notes so you can listen while in the car, working out, or simply sitting at your desk. Ask a friend to quiz you from your flashcards, or try teaching someone the material to solidify it in your mind.

STEP 4: CREATE YOUR ENVIRONMENT

It's important to avoid distractions while you study. This includes both the obvious distractions like visitors and the subtle distractions like an uncomfortable chair (or a too-comfortable couch that makes you want to fall asleep). Set up the best study environment possible: good lighting and a comfortable work area. If background music helps you focus, you may want to turn it on, but otherwise keep the room quiet. If you are using a computer to take notes, be sure you don't have any other windows open, especially applications like social media, games, or anything else that could distract you. Silence your phone and turn off notifications. Be sure to keep water close by so you stay hydrated while you study (but avoid unhealthy drinks and snacks).

Also, take into account the best time of day to study. Are you freshest first thing in the morning? Try to set aside some time then to work through the material. Is your mind clearer in the afternoon or evening? Schedule your study session then. Another method is to study at the same time of day that you will take the test, so that your brain gets used to working on the material at that time and will be ready to focus at test time.

STEP 5: STUDY!

Once you have done all the study preparation, it's time to settle into the actual studying. Sit down, take a few moments to settle your mind so you can focus, and begin to follow your study plan. Don't give in to distractions or let yourself procrastinate. This is your time to prepare so you'll be ready to fearlessly approach the test. Make the most of the time and stay focused.

Of course, you don't want to burn out. If you study too long you may find that you're not retaining the information very well. Take regular study breaks. For example, taking five minutes out of every hour to walk briskly, breathing deeply and swinging your arms, can help your mind stay fresh.

As you get to the end of each chapter or section, it's a good idea to do a quick review. Remind yourself of what you learned and work on any difficult parts. When you feel that you've mastered the material, move on to the next part. At the end of your study session, briefly skim through your notes again.

But while review is helpful, cramming last minute is NOT. If at all possible, work ahead so that you won't need to fit all your study into the last day. Cramming overloads your brain with more information than it can process and retain, and your tired mind may struggle to recall even previously learned information when it is overwhelmed with last-minute study. Also, the urgent nature of cramming and the stress placed on your brain contribute to anxiety. You'll be more likely to go to the test feeling unprepared and having trouble thinking clearly.

So don't cram, and don't stay up late before the test, even just to review your notes at a leisurely pace. Your brain needs rest more than it needs to go over the information again. In fact, plan to finish your studies by noon or early afternoon the day before the test. Give your brain the rest of the day to relax or focus on other things, and get a good night's sleep. Then you will be fresh for the test and better able to recall what you've studied.

STEP 6: TAKE A PRACTICE TEST

Many courses offer sample tests, either online or in the study materials. This is an excellent resource to check whether you have mastered the material, as well as to prepare for the test format and environment.

Check the test format ahead of time: the number of questions, the type (multiple choice, free response, etc.), and the time limit. Then create a plan for working through them. For example, if you have 30 minutes to take a 60-question test, your limit is 30 seconds per question. Spend less time on the questions you know well so that you can take more time on the difficult ones.

If you have time to take several practice tests, take the first one open book, with no time limit. Work through the questions at your own pace and make sure you fully understand them. Gradually work up to taking a test under test conditions: sit at a desk with all study materials put away and set a timer. Pace yourself to make sure you finish the test with time to spare and go back to check your answers if you have time.

After each test, check your answers. On the questions you missed, be sure you understand why you missed them. Did you misread the question (tests can use tricky wording)? Did you forget the information? Or was it something you hadn't learned? Go back and study any shaky areas that the practice tests reveal.

Taking these tests not only helps with your grade, but also aids in combating test anxiety. If you're already used to the test conditions, you're less likely to worry about it, and working through tests until you're scoring well gives you a confidence boost. Go through the practice tests until you feel comfortable, and then you can go into the test knowing that you're ready for it.

Test Tips

On test day, you should be confident, knowing that you've prepared well and are ready to answer the questions. But aside from preparation, there are several test day strategies you can employ to maximize your performance.

First, as stated before, get a good night's sleep the night before the test (and for several nights before that, if possible). Go into the test with a fresh, alert mind rather than staying up late to study.

Try not to change too much about your normal routine on the day of the test. It's important to eat a nutritious breakfast, but if you normally don't eat breakfast at all, consider eating just a protein bar. If you're a coffee drinker, go ahead and have your normal coffee. Just make sure you time it so that the caffeine doesn't wear off right in the middle of your test. Avoid sugary beverages, and drink enough water to stay hydrated but not so much that you need a restroom break 10 minutes into the test. If your test isn't first thing in the morning, consider going for a walk or doing a light workout before the test to get your blood flowing.

Allow yourself enough time to get ready, and leave for the test with plenty of time to spare so you won't have the anxiety of scrambling to arrive in time. Another reason to be early is to select a good seat. It's helpful to sit away from doors and windows, which can be distracting. Find a good seat, get out your supplies, and settle your mind before the test begins.

When the test begins, start by going over the instructions carefully, even if you already know what to expect. Make sure you avoid any careless mistakes by following the directions.

Then begin working through the questions, pacing yourself as you've practiced. If you're not sure on an answer, don't spend too much time on it, and don't let it shake your confidence. Either skip it and come back later, or eliminate as many wrong answers as possible and guess among the remaining ones. Don't dwell on these questions as you continue—put them out of your mind and focus on what lies ahead.

Be sure to read all of the answer choices, even if you're sure the first one is the right answer. Sometimes you'll find a better one if you keep reading. But don't second-guess yourself if you do immediately know the answer. Your gut instinct is usually right. Don't let test anxiety rob you of the information you know.

If you have time at the end of the test (and if the test format allows), go back and review your answers. Be cautious about changing any, since your first instinct tends to be correct, but make sure you didn't misread any of the questions or accidentally mark the wrong answer choice. Look over any you skipped and make an educated guess.

At the end, leave the test feeling confident. You've done your best, so don't waste time worrying about your performance or wishing you could change anything. Instead, celebrate the successful completion of this test. And finally, use this test to learn how to deal with anxiety even better next time.

> **Review Video: Test Anxiety**
> Visit mometrix.com/academy and enter code: 100340

Important Qualification

Not all anxiety is created equal. If your test anxiety is causing major issues in your life beyond the classroom or testing center, or if you are experiencing troubling physical symptoms related to your anxiety, it may be a sign of a serious physiological or psychological condition. If this sounds like your situation, we strongly encourage you to seek professional help.

Online Resources

Due to our efforts to try to keep this book to a manageable length, we've created a link that will give you access to all of your online resources:

mometrix.com/resources719/dsstlsdevpsy